THE PARISH IN TRANSITION

PROCEEDINGS OF A CONFERENCE ON THE AMERICAN CATHOLIC PARISH

May 1985

David Byers
Editor

Sponsored by
Foundations and Donors Interested in Catholic Activities, Inc.

In association with
Bishops' Committee on Priestly Life and Ministry
National Conference of Catholic Bishops
Institute for Pastoral and Social Ministry
University of Notre Dame
Lilly Endowment, Inc.
National Pastoral Life Center

In keeping with its mission to encourage the priesthood and parochial ministries, the NCCB Committee on Priestly Life and Ministry, through its Secretariat, communicates the proceedings of "The American Catholic Parish in Transition," a symposium held in conjunction with Foundations and Donors Interested in Catholic Activities, Inc., May 29–30, 1985. This present document, *The Parish in Transition*, contains the proceedings of that symposium. The text was reviewed by Rev. Msgr. Colin A. MacDonald, Executive Director of the Secretariat for Priestly Life and Ministry, and has been authorized for publication by the undersigned.

Monsignor Daniel F. Hoye
General Secretary
NCCB/USCC

November 18, 1985

FADICA
Foundations and Donors Interested in Catholic Activities, Inc.

Organized in 1976, FADICA is an effort among a growing number of private foundations and donors across the country and in Europe to establish contact and maintain communication with one another. In addition to facilitating the exchange of information among its members, FADICA serves as a forum for the discussion of common grant requests and programs of mutual interest, as a means of coordinating joint efforts by member foundations, and as a way to keep its members abreast of recent developments in the Church.

Notre Dame Study of Catholic Parish Life, extract from "Report 1," December 1984, by David C. Leege and Joseph Gremillion; and *Notre Dame Study of Catholic Parish Life*, extract from "Report 2," February 1985, by Jay Dolan and David C. Leege, used with permission of the Study of Catholic Parish Life, University of Notre Dame, Notre Dame, Indiana.

Copyright © 1986
United States Catholic Conference, Inc.
1312 Massachusetts Avenue, N.W.
Washington, D.C. 20005-4105
All rights reserved.

CONTENTS

Preface 1

Introduction 3

The American Catholic Parish of the 1980s 7

The American Catholic Parish
A Historical Perspective, 1820–1980 33

Pastors: Challenges and Expectations
in a Time of Change 47

Parish Leadership 57

The Parish at Worship 73

Appendix I
Welcome and Conclusion 97

Appendix II
The U.S. Parish Twenty Years after Vatican II:
An Introduction to the Study 105

PREFACE

Presenting the proceedings of a conference in written form requires balance. One does not want to lose the sense of spontaneity and interaction that marked the meeting. On the other hand, people speak much more diffusely than they write. In order to produce a book that presents its subject coherently and without waste of words, the editor finds himself paring sentences, rearranging material, and deleting the occasional clever but irrelevant remark.

Of the five central chapters of the book, four are amalgams. The first part of each chapter is a major presentation based on the Notre Dame Study of Catholic Parish Life; the subsequent material consists of reactions from panel members and, in some instances, members of the audience. I have not identified those who rose to question or comment from the floor, on the grounds that too many names would only confuse the reader. The principal speaker and the panel members, if any, are listed on the half-title page of each chapter for easy reference, and their comments are labelled by name in the text.

The Introduction offers a brief account of the conference itself and of its primary sponsor, Foundations and Donors Interested in Catholic Activities, Inc. (FADICA). Chapter four is a speech based on a survey of Chicago pastors. Appendix I offers the Welcome and Conclusion, which record portions of the opening and closing sessions of the conference. Finally, Appendix II discusses the scope and method of the Notre Dame Study of Catholic Parish Life.

I would like to acknowledge the valuable help of Dr. Francis Butler, president of FADICA, who coordinated the collection of the materials and acted as liaison with contributing scholars.

David Byers
Editor

INTRODUCTION

According to the findings of the Notre Dame Study of Catholic Parish Life—the most extensive study ever conducted of Catholic parishes in America—there is good news and bad news about contemporary parish life.

Some of the good news.

Lay participation in the parish is great and growing. Nearly half of all parishioners engage in some parish activity in addition to Mass, and 83% of the leadership consists of laypeople.

The Catholic Church is no longer simply an urban, immigrant institution. More than one-third of all adult Catholics live in cities of less than 50,000, in small towns, and in the countryside.

Sixty-three percent of parishes offer adult religious education programs, suggesting that Catholics associate their religion with a lifelong learning process.

Among Catholics who attend Mass weekly, 80% receive Communion.

Fifty-two percent of the members of parish councils are women, as are 58% of the most influential parish leaders.

More than 85% of those the study polled "feel that their parish meets their spiritual needs."

Some of the bad news.

About 44% of Catholics attend Mass regularly. Twenty-seven percent of the adults attend once a year or not at all, a figure that rises to 34% for those under the age of 30.

Thirty-five percent of active parishioners go to confession once a year, only 6% go once a month or more. Fifteen percent of volunteer parish leaders never go to confession; neither do 38% of active parishioners under 30.

Although 75% of parishes have parish councils, only 4% of the pastors interviewed identified the council as one of the five most influential factors in parish life.

Forty-six percent of parishes have prayer and reflection groups, but only 32% have evangelization programs, and these outward-looking programs involve less than half of one percent of all parishioners.

While more than one-third of adult Catholics are single, parochial programs tend to gear their programs to traditional family units. Perhaps as a result, young singles remain relatively uninvolved in parish activities, with the exception of liturgy planning and music.

The present volume contains much more news about the parish. It represents the edited proceedings of a conference held in Chicago May 29–30, 1985. The purpose of the conference was to present and discuss the early results of a three-year study on parish life conducted by the Institute for Pastoral and Social Ministry and the Center for the Study of

Man in Contemporary Society, both of which are located at the University of Notre Dame. The study was underwritten by a major grant from the Lilly Endowment.

Foundations and Donors Interested in Catholic Activities, Inc. (FADICA) sponsored the symposium in association with the Committee on Priestly Life and Ministry of the National Conference of Catholic Bishops, the University of Notre Dame, the National Pastoral Life Center, and the Lilly Endowment, Inc. The conference, attended by more than 100 people, brought together foundation representatives and scholars with pastors, parish staff personnel, parish council members, and lay volunteers from around the country. Entitled "The American Catholic Parish in Transition," it provided a forum for presenting data drawn from the Notre Dame study on the history of the parish, the broad characteristics of parish life in the 1980s, parish leadership, and parish spirituality.

The principal sessions of the conference were organized around these topics. Each was designed to promote give-and-take between a major speaker on the one hand and a panel and/or members of the audience on the other. This book, then, provides both information and starting points for discussing the issues the Notre Dame data raise. While further analysis will clarify many aspects of contemporary parish life, the data offer ecclesiastical planners, parish leaders, and the faithful at large provocative insights into the present and future of Catholicism in America.

Contrary to popular belief, foundations are not the main source of philanthropy in America. A recent report of the Council on Foundations notes that organized religion donates much more money each year than all of the 23,000 private foundations combined. Indeed, these foundations accounted for only five percent of the $60 billion charitable dollars given in 1984. Foundation funds for religious purposes are even more limited. Of the 4,000 largest foundations in the United States, less than 400 give to religious causes. Even fewer have any interest in the Catholic Church.

This was the context for the founding of Foundations and Donors Interested in Catholic Activities, Inc. in 1976. FADICA provides services to assist its 35 members in allocating their grant funds responsibly and well. FADICA's usefulness derives not just from the $50 million these members distribute annually, but also from the educational experiences it provides and the catalytic role it plays in bringing groups and individuals together around significant trends and problems affecting Catholic life. Working with experts and Catholic leaders, FADICA people explore how best to respond to these concerns.

FADICA's symposia often provide opportunity to the Church's "pastoral entrepreneurs," the creative men and women who discern a need and have a promising idea, but lack the means to carry it out. Through FADICA, these visionaries come face to face with scholars, decision makers, and funders who, working together, can give that promising idea substance. The RENEW program that has brought new vitality to so many dioceses is one example of this collaboration.

Though the interests of its members are diverse, FADICA has promoted cooperative effort in several key areas. Some examples:

Communications. When FADICA became concerned that the newly created Catholic Telecommunications Network of America (CTNA) was in jeopardy, some members made matching grant money available to dioceses to purchase receiving equipment. As a result, at least 25 new dioceses have become CTNA affiliates since the program started in 1984. At the same time, FADICA members helped launch NEWSFRONT, a weekly program of religious news currently airing on PBS.

Future Church Leadership. Working with the Catholic bishops, FADICA convened an extensive national discussion of the crisis in priestly and religious vocations. A national task force was subsequently formed to make recommendations to the bishops and the Catholic Vocations Council.

Education. FADICA members have assisted the National Catholic Educational Association in studying the values and faith commitment of lay teachers in Catholic high schools.

Parish Life. FADICA sees the revitalization of the parish as critical to the future of the Church in this country. Besides the effort represented by this volume, FADICA has assisted in the establishment of the National Pastoral Life Center and the promotion of parish renewal efforts.

FADICA does not accept grant proposals, nor does it serve as a contact between grantseekers and any of its members. The organization has published *Foundation Guide for Religious Grantseekers,* second edition, which is available from Scholars Press for $11.95.

Although the giving programs of all FADICA's members may pale in comparison with the billion-dollar-plus annual contribution of rank-and-file Catholics, its members have learned that through collaboration, constant study, and dialogue, they can improve their own effectiveness and help shape the Church of the future. In a recent essay on Catholic philanthropy, the distinguished historian Msgr. John Tracy Ellis remarks:

> FADICA may be seen as a late twentieth-century reflection of the generally prosperous society that gave it birth. It represents a genuine Christian effort to strengthen and improve the Church's life in the United States in a way commensurate with its present needs.

THE AMERICAN CATHOLIC PARISH OF THE 1980s

SPEAKER

Dr. David C. Leege
Director, Center for the Study of Contemporary Society
University of Notre Dame

PANEL

Rev. Philip J. Murnion
Director, National Pastoral Life Center

Sr. Kathleen Hughes, RSCJ
Professor of Liturgy, Catholic Theological Union

Sr. Doris Gottmoeller, RSM
Provincial Administrator, Sisters of Mercy
Cincinnati

Mr. Harry A. Fagan
Associate Director, National Pastoral Life Center

Rev. Brian T. Joyce
Pastor, St. Monica's Parish
Moraga, California

The early reports from the Notre Dame Study of Catholic Parish Life have outlined the methods and techniques of the study and have set the stage for interpreting the findings. Today I would like to offer some caveats about the proper use of the study, to focus attention on some of the most significant characteristics of American Catholics in their parishes, and to suggest some policy concerns for which these findings are relevant.

What can we expect from the Notre Dame study? What are its strengths and limitations?

The study is a reasonably comprehensive, systematic, comparative, and cross-disciplinary look at the American Catholic parish 20 years after Vatican II. Through empirical research social scientists have learned a great deal about religious values and religious organizations over the last three decades. Some of the best work has been based on national or regional probability samples and has used survey research methods. Such studies permit trustworthy generalizations about Catholics or members of other religious bodies. Even though they do not meet strict probability sampling assumptions—nowhere is there a list of all Catholics in the United States from which to draw samples with known probabilities of selection—nevertheless, pooled samples of Catholics from successive surveys approximate scientific samples sufficiently that we can be confident about their use. The General Social Surveys of the National Opinion Research Center are of this kind. The GSS, as they are called, or their predecessors have been conducted for two decades, are well known to the media, and are highly respected by scholars.

While our study makes use of GSS data, especially when we want to generalize about all adult Catholics, the specific samples we generated are different by design from these data. The Notre Dame study is based on the assumption that people do not exist in the abstract, but exist within specific social contexts. These social contexts condition values and attitudes. When we want to study religious contexts among Catholics, it is reasonable to look at life within their parishes. While primary religious socialization occurs within the family, the parish is often shaped by its member families, just as it is the shaper of those families. Therefore, we had to develop a sampling design that could yield a reasonably large number of parishes for comparative purposes, but was sufficiently small to be studied through identical research techniques by similarly trained people. We wanted those techniques to yield perceptions of interactions among pastor, paid staff, volunteer leaders, and ordinary parishioners. We wanted those techniques to yield observations of common but central events in the parish, especially the Sunday liturgies. And just as no person exists in a social vacuum, so no parish exists in a historical vacuum. Thus, we wanted to generate historical data, both about that parish and more generally about the other parishes in its diocese and region.

Our research design began with the collection of data on a large scientific sample of 1,100 U.S. parishes. Once we analyzed that data and knew the dimensions upon which parishes differed most significantly, we could classify the large sample according to these dimensions, and draw a smaller sample of 36 parishes that were representative of these dimensions. We submitted these 36 parishes to intensive analysis. Within these parishes we could identify the leaders by a variety of techniques and survey them, and we could draw disproportionate probability samples of rank-and-file parishioners in such a way that the sample size was always large enough to generalize within each parish with confidence. When we want to generalize across parish lines we have to weight each parishioner to his or her proper proportion among all Catholics carried on the membership rolls in these parishes. This design allows us to examine the internal dynamics of parishes, and at the same time to generalize about parishioners.

The Catholic parish life sample does not allow us to generalize about *all* adult Catholics in the United States, however. We have surveyed core Catholics with parish connections. Many Catholics, perhaps between one-fourth and one-third, do not have parish connections. They attend Mass sporadically or not at all. They may live in a parish but not be listed on the parish census rolls. Or they may be on the rolls, but remain so uninterested in parish life that they ignore our repeated efforts to survey their views.

Remarkably, 59% of those we surveyed took the time to fill out our lengthy questionnaire. We suspect that our parish-connected sample is older, more female, and somewhat more conservative on policy questions than would be found on a probability sample of all Catholics in the United States. We cannot be sure because there is no list of all adult Catholics and, therefore, no sample survey using the same questions against which to compare our findings.

Because we have purposely designed our intensive samples to measure the internal dynamics of the parish and the contextual effects, those findings that compare Catholics in different types of parishes will be of greatest interest. We have excluded Hispanic parishes from the intensive studies for a variety of cultural and methodological reasons. Hispanics, a heterogeneous population that may have grown into one-fourth of the Church in the United States, need to be studied using distinctive methods. Hopefully, such a study can be undertaken in the future.

To summarize: the Notre Dame data permit us to generalize about all Catholic parishes in the United States, not all Catholics in the United States. We are restricted to generalizing about core non-Hispanic Catholics, both within and across parish lines. When we generalize about all adult Catholics, active and inactive, we are using data from outside the present study. When we put parishes under a microscope and examine their internal dynamics, we are using our representative sample of 36 parishes.

My final caveat centers on differences in the professional mandates of social scientists and church policy makers. For social scientists the isolated datum is of little interest. It is the pattern of the general relationship that must be understood. Thus, for example, it is of passing curiosity to me that 58% of those listed as among the most influential in their parish are women. That alone is not convincing evidence about the leadership role of women in the contemporary parish. What is important is the entire battery of theoretically based predictions that in some ministries women will predominate. In other ministries, men will be more prominent. When the pattern of predictions is upheld, and multiple pieces of evidence converge on the same finding, when the evidence is gathered through different methods, then that finding is of interest to social scientists.

Policy makers, managers, and newspaper reporters, on the other hand, have other legitimate purposes. Policy makers and managers of churches look for the finding that represents behaviors or attitudes that can be altered through their intervention, through their leadership. For example, if in a lengthy interpretation of confession and communal penance, it is shown in a sentence or two that the proportion of parishioners making private confession is highest when only rite one is available and lowest when only rite three is available and the policy maker is trying to encourage private confession, then he is tempted to conclude that communal penance rites should be discontinued. Overlooked, however, may be a lengthy argument and some evidence that the offering of communal penance rites may bring Catholics who would never confess under rite one much closer to the Church's sacraments.

Responsible communication between social scientists and church leaders is not easy. When it suits their personal agendas for the Church, both sides will use isolated social scientific findings as weapons, with all the force of dogmatic theology. Sometimes social scientists will fail to anticipate how a finding may be misused and contribute to great mischief in the life of the Church. Sometimes church policy makers may attribute too much authority to our findings because they bear the name Notre Dame.

We, of course, are ultimately responsible for shortcomings, and we pray that the spirit of the Lord will grant us a full measure of openness and patience. That is the reason for meetings like this one. You can help point out and overcome some of our limitations. We will continue to use many consultants to critique our reports. If our reporting schedule is delayed at times by these procedures, so be it. It is better to publish proper material that will not be misused than to get analysis out hurriedly and do harm in the Church.

Asking what American Catholics look like today is like asking a geologist to describe the Earth's features. American Catholics are very heterogeneous, but the majority have now entered the American mainstream and the educated middle class. Catholics are found decreasingly in ethnic enclaves. The immigrant parish with its emphases on devotional pieties, parochial education for the children, passive liturgies, a plentitude of vocations, and hierarchical leadership is giving way to the post-Vatican II parish with biblically oriented adult education, participatory liturgies, a scarcity of priests and religious, and ministries and governance shared by the laity. When the Church began to view itself as the people of God following the Second Vatican Council, it found an American Catholic laity with many of the advantages of education and with middle-class attitudes that made it ready to assume responsibility.

The greatest leaps upward in education came between the Second World War and the mid-1970s. By any criterion of educational mobility, Catholics outpaced every other religious group during that period. But when you begin well behind the starting blocks, you have a longer race to run. And the competition does not stand still. Thus, although the mobility data from the 1960s and 1970s hinted that non-Hispanic Catholics would soon become the most well-educated sector of the American populace, the average educational attainment of adult Catholics in the mid-1980s, while above that of Methodists, Lutherans, and Baptists, is still slightly below that of Jews, Episcopalians, and Presbyterians. This phenomenon is partly regional; more Catholics are in the Northeast, more Protestants are in the South.

So much attention has been paid to mobility, however, that analysts have not emphasized the implications of two other features in the educational attainment data. First, the second- and even third-generation college student is now becoming the norm in many non-Hispanic Catholic families. In the 1950s and early 1960s American colleges and universities took in many young Catholics who were among the first generation of their family to attend college. Prior to that time, most Catholic young people had to go to work or to war after high school—if they finished at all. They took on adult responsibilities for wage earning and parenting at an early age. Since they moved into a relatively fixed class system, their parish connections remained stable. Now that Catholic families are into the second and third college generation, however, we must recognize that the period of economic dependency on parents is longer, even though children may become geographically separated from their parents earlier. Their old parish connections are often first interrupted for college and then virtually severed as young people move into the first job and apartment, and much later take on marital responsibilities. The normal age of first marriage is pushed back because it takes longer to finish college and perhaps professional school. It takes longer to get settled in the right white-collar or professional position. Given these widespread destabilizing forces, the remarkable phenomenon is not the decline in Mass attendance among educated young Catholics, but the relatively high attendance level.

The second factor hidden by the emphasis on educational mobility is a simple matter of baby booms and birth rates. Contrary to stereotypes, American Catholics of child-bearing age have not always and do not presently have the largest families. The post-World War II baby boom hit Protestant families sooner than it did Catholics, and the average number of children in families of Protestants now in their 60s is actually slightly higher than in the families of Catholics of the same age. But Catholics now in their 40s and 50s had much larger families than Protestants. That baby boom has created a bulge in the Catholic population, so that 4% more of the Catholic population is between 18 and 29 than of the Protestant population.

Therein lies one of the reasons why Catholics are currently disproportionately represented in the enrollment figures of American colleges and universities. One report says that Catholics, while 25% of the U.S. population, make up 40% of those enrolled in college. Another reason is that mothers of the baby boom generation with children out of the nest feel they have to catch up with other college-educated women they know. They are among the growing nontraditional-age student population.

Regardless of what interpretation one accepts, the results are the same. American Catholics are far more educated than they ever were. Women are pursuing education just as are men in all fields. Both men and women have greater skills to offer their parishes. Their expectations of parish ministries and programs have probably increased. Finally, they have often experienced many years without stable roots in a parish due to residential mobility.

The implications of these social characteristics for the Church's ordained leadership at the parish level and above are obvious. Many lay members, male and female, have as much or more education than do priests or bishops. The legitimacy accorded church authority is no longer traditional, but increasingly rational. Catholics have known both education and life away from ancestral parishes; they are accustomed in their jobs and daily life to means-ends calculations and often have to be won to the reasonableness of church policy. They live in a society and have been socialized through an American educational system that seldom accords absolute authority to any human being. They are accustomed to owing loyalty to an institution while still questioning specific policies of its leaders. They find no great inconsistency in accepting the central mysteries of the Church and rejecting some of its more recent teachings. Finally, they often possess as varied skills for parish service as do priests or religious.

The American emphasis on voluntarism tells today's Catholics that those skills should be used and that they should be consulted on program planning at the parish level. They are also very pragmatic when it comes to policy. Having either never known a submissive life of devotional piety, or having replaced it with active post-Vatican II Trinitarian theology and a people of God imagery, they are sufficiently confident of their own faculties and the presence of the spirit of Christ to confront crises with basic policy changes. We see evidence of that in Project 1990 here in Chicago, where lay leaders appear quite willing after some study of the matter to accept married priests.

One aspect of American Catholic demographics is easily misunderstood. We have found from analysis of GSS data that around the late

1970s a significant change in family size was occurring. The National Center for Health Statistics has found that birth rates have changed so that white Catholics are now having fewer children than white Protestants. We do not know whether Catholics are simply marrying later and will eventually equal or surpass Protestants in family size, but their birth rate is lower at the present time.

There is a risk of misinterpreting this finding. Some people automatically assume that fewer children per family will lead to a decline in the size of the next generation of Catholics. Not at all. Since there are more young Catholics of child-bearing age nowadays as a result of the earlier baby boom, even if they have smaller families than Protestants, the total number of Catholics will either continue to grow or remain about the same. Thus, any notion that there will be less need for parochial schools, CCD, youth ministries, family counseling services, and so on one decade hence must be quickly dismissed. The children and their families will be there to be served, even if birth rates decline among the products of the earlier baby boom.

Analyses of income and social-class data from GSS for the 1960s and 1970s argued that after Jews, non-Hispanic Catholics had attained the highest average annual family income among American church groups. That was quite a surprise to many ethnic Catholics who for years had operated with an underdog psychology. The GSS data for the 1980s, however, suggest that non-Hispanic Catholics are closer to the middle of the pack. Jews, Presbyterians, and Episcopalians still have higher family incomes than Catholics; Methodists, Lutherans, and Baptists are lower. However, this finding appears to be primarily the result of the bulge of the Catholic population in the 18 to 29 age bracket. These people have a decade or two to go before reaching their maximum earning potential.

Contrasted with young Protestants, young non-Hispanic Catholics are staying in school a bit longer, appear to be pursuing higher paying jobs early and are settling into marriage and parenthood later. Unless the boardroom is somehow barred to Catholics, we can anticipate that as the baby bulge works its way through the life cycle, non-Hispanic Catholics will indeed be at the top of the economic ladder within a decade or two.

The political consequences of these demographic developments are evident, within both the Church and the larger society. Many Catholics have grasped economic power and learned political savvy. While the plurality of non-Hispanic Catholics still call themselves Democrats, their ideology has tilted decidedly to the right. In fact, the entire country has shifted to the right during the last decade. Catholics still trail this shift by about seven percentage points, but it is gathering momentum, particularly in the baby bulge generation, those 18 to 29 years old. There are apt to be pronounced differences among the New Deal liberalism of Catholics over 50, the ideological liberalism of Catholics in their 30s and 40s, and the acquisitive conservatism of Catholics under 30. On major public policy issues, Catholics have about as many different viewpoints as France has wines. When leaders of the Church speak to public issues, other

Catholics can commandeer the "bully pulpits" and find receptive audiences for contrary opinions. We have seen it in the response to recent pastoral letters. Lay Catholics have the same potential for reacting against the economic teachings of pope and bishops in the 1980s as lay Protestants had for reacting against the civil rights efforts of their leaders in the 1960s.

There are three aspects of American Catholicism that we tend to overlook. First, about 30% of American Catholics do not reside in the great urban centers where culture and the public agenda are shaped. They live in small towns, in unincorporated areas, on farms. We think of Baptists and Methodists as rural and small-town people and of Catholics as urban. But the total Catholic rural and small-town population is as large as the total membership of the Baptist or Methodist Churches, and larger than the combined Lutheran Churches. This population covers the spectrum from foreclosed farmers to rich ranchers, from minimum-wage laborers to well-paid professionals. A description that portrays only the immigrant church of the cities and the middle-class church of the suburbs misses a large part of the American Catholic community.

We must also pay attention to the Hispanics and the Asians. The ancestors of many Hispanics were within the Church in the United States well before most of us other Catholics were. Most Hispanics today, however, are recent immigrants. While they share a single language, they are many peoples with great cultural diversity. They are as different from one another as the Chicago physician who migrated from Cuba and comes from a ruling-caste Spanish family is from the migrant Mexican-American farm worker who descended from American Indians or the black Dominican taxi driver whose ancestors were African slaves. Our Church is also their Church. The Hispanics are beginning to come of age in America. Consider the forecast that before the turn of the century, over half of all Catholics in Chicago will be Hispanic or non-white. Asians, as ethnically and culturally varied as the Hispanics, are also increasingly evident in parishes all over the country. In the five-county Los Angeles metropolitan area, one estimate says that 40% of the adults are foreign-born. Most of these people are Hispanic or Asian, and at least 80% of them are thought to be Catholic. Just at a time when the dominant element in American Catholicism is white, well educated and middle class, we become aware that large parts of this Church are not white, not well educated, and not middle class.

Finally, we often forget that many Catholics over the age of 35 remain rooted in the old immigrant experience. They were either partially or completely socialized by that constellation of values and practices associated with the immigrant parish. In the rush of change we sometimes forget the persistence of memory, both personal and communal. Just as my father clung to the certainty that the language of heaven is German, so the 60-year-old parishioner feels deep bewilderment at the failure of her parish to practice a corporate devotion to its patron saint. It would be difficult to convince this faithful Catholic that there is a greater sense of community in the congregational hymns, responses, and other forms of liturgical participation than there was in the silent devotion practiced in her youth. Is it any wonder that the road to liturgical change has been rocky?

So that is what we are: white, urban, educated, middle class, participatory, powerful, pragmatic; and, at the same time, tan, black, yellow, rural, working in necessary but demeaning tasks, on the outside looking in, nostalgic for devotions past. If these are American Catholics, can you think of any more complicated task than planning for the American parish? But the very genius of a church, as opposed to a denomination or a sect, is that it learns how to celebrate and sanctify cultural diversities and social differences. Let us briefly examine the interplay of some of these characteristics of American Catholics and the characteristics of their parishes.

Catholic parishes are very large. The average parish serves about 2,300 people, and about 15% serve 5,000 or more. Interestingly enough, the average number of Catholics in a parish has increased over the past five years and so has attendance at Mass. When contrasted with parishes in Catholic countries elsewhere, American parishes are still rather small. But, the average Catholic will compare his parish with nearby Protestant congregations, and it is almost always larger.

Most Catholics now realize there is a serious shortage of priests and religious. Slightly over one-half of American parishes are served by one full-time priest; a little over one-quarter of the parishes have two full-time priests; about one in seven has three full-time priests. About one-third of the parishes have access to a part-time priest. The average age of priests continues to push upward, yet there is no bulge of young candidates for the priesthood to match the bulge in the young Catholic population. If the average number of Catholics per parish is over 2,300, it is sobering to note that the average number of full-time priests per parish is 1.7. This is a better ratio of priests to laity than is found in most Catholic countries, but it is well under the ratio of Protestant pastors to laity in the United States. But, participation in Mass and parish programs is much higher here than in Belgium, France, or Italy, where as much as 85% of the people simply don't practice their religion.

Vocations to religious orders have also declined precipitously. Our data attest to the unavailability and the increasing age of sisters and brothers.

Someone has to pick up the slack. The laity are trying. In parish after parish we find a cadre of laypersons who volunteer nearly as many hours to parish service as the pastor or paid staff is contributing. These volunteers, whether they be in ministries of nurture or mercy, liturgy or governance, are disproportionately women. Since American Catholics are educated and are products of cultural values that encourage pragmatism, voluntarism, participation, and responsibility, the laity do not feel the need for special charisms to fill roles formerly filled by priests or religious. When asked about the essential feature of the priest's role, by a wide margin parishioners said it is bound up in the celebration of Mass and the sacraments. It appears that they would be comfortable sharing (or taking over) virtually all other aspects of his work. When asked to rank the trait they most value in a pastor, parishioners named sensitivity to the needs of others by a wide margin over holiness, learning, good preaching skills, good organizing skills, or anything else. They want a pastor who understands them, who consults them, who respects them as contributors to the common life of the parish.

A large proportion of core Catholics—about 85%—seem comfortable with the idea that they will attend the parish within whose boundaries they reside, although they will occasionally participate in a Mass elsewhere. (Once again, bear in mind that *core Catholics* are those with definite parish connections.) Interestingly, the reason people cite most often for attending a given parish, beyond geographical location, is not its style of liturgy or acceptance of Vatican II reforms, but the quality of pastoral care. *Pastoral care* refers not just to the actions of a priest, but often to those of an entire team made up of priest, religious, and laity; *pastor* is becoming a corporate term in this country. This is perhaps another reason why people look for a sensitive priest. They want someone who can work with a leadership team of staff and volunteers, while at the same time appreciating the needs and gifts of ordinary parishioners.

About 85% of the core parishioners express the view that their parish satisfies their religious needs, while only 45% feel that it meets their social needs. The suburban parish—typically the largest parish in our sample—was least likely to meet social needs. Yet that does not seem to matter to many suburban Catholics. Those most satisfied with the parish as a social unit are the highly active people who volunteer for a wide variety of ministries and programs. Those who claim the parish fails to meet their social needs do not assign great priority to improving the social life of their parish, because they feel its primary purpose is religious enrichment. In the functionally specialized suburbs, then, many Catholics want little more out of the Church than a satisfying religious life; they conduct their social life elsewhere. It is quite the opposite in the small towns where parishioners place heavy social demands on their parishes. Curiously, despite the size of parishes, only one in eight has made a conscious effort to organize parish subdivisions or smaller communities within the parish.

In some ways, parishes are failing to keep pace with the changing needs of their parishioners. Despite the fact that about 25% of adult Catholics who have ever married have experienced divorce or separation, only 20% of the parishes have programs for divorced Catholics. On a wide variety of survey indicators, core Catholics told us that the Church needs to understand better the nature of contemporary American life. In fact, there is a decidedly this-worldly rather than otherworldly cast to the programmatic priorities of core Catholics. For example, not only would they like their parishes to offer more effective service when marriages are in trouble, but they would also like to get better help on some of the things that make marriages go on the rocks—alcoholism and substance abuse, economic problems, and so on.

Almost all respondents give high priority to religious formation programs for children and teens; virtually all parishes have such programs. On the other hand, while a sizeable proportion want more attention paid to adult religious education, only a little over 60% of the parishes have some kind of adult education program. It should come as no surprise that educated Catholic laypeople will want to continue their religious education just as they have their regular education. They will seek bible study groups, prayer groups, or religious discussions in nearby Protestant churches or ecumenical neighborhood groups if they can't find such opportunities in the parish. Finally, despite the obvious need for increasing lay responsibility for parish ministries, only about one-fourth of the parishes have organized lay leadership training programs. By and large, diocesan programs do not yet penetrate to the parish level. One sign of hope is that about one-third of all parishes have followed some version of a formal parish renewal program. Often the need for lay leadership training is recognized during renewal.

Many patterns of leadership are emerging. Some involve parish councils, but often the council is not the most important component of the leadership network. While 76% of parishes have a council, parishes have also evolved other strategies for policy planning and review: congregational assemblies, elected executive committees, functionally specialized boards, surveys, and so on. Regardless of the structure of governance, our studies clearly show that laypersons expect to participate in it. No parishes are in deeper trouble, based on measures of identification and loyalty, than those where lay involvement in formal liturgical roles and in parish governance is suppressed. It is not that laity want to dominate. They simply want to be heard and to be affirmed as responsible members of a community.

Our studies of influence within the parish community generally show that those performing a ministry have the greatest voice in parish planning and policy. Disproportionately, it is women who are conducting the ministries and thereby gaining influence. Moreover, influence is becoming less centralized and formal. Position and structure alone no longer tell the story of parish governance.

One other suggestion emerges from the data. There is a tendency toward recognizing lay responsibility through providing credentials to graduates of training programs. Thus, there is a credentialed liturgist or a credentialed minister of adult education or a credentialed minister to the sick. Some pastors and leaders are seeing, however, that these programs give individuals such a distinctive set of skills that they intimidate other parishioners, creating new splits in the parish. Just as the priest has had to learn how to be sensitive, so the credentialed lay minister must remember that the parish is a people of God that must be encouraged and affirmed. Otherwise, we have merely traded a hierarchical dominance based on ordination for one based on training credentials.

Pastors wonder: "Where is this mythical parish where so many laypersons want to serve? In my experience, it is always the same old people." Nothing is more clear from the patterns of recruitment in our leadership sample than that people may want to serve but are shy in offering their services. Our data for volunteer leaders show that 68% had to be asked to participate. Once asked, once encouraged, once affirmed, once shown "how to," however, they take on responsibility after responsibility. One of the challenges of pastoring is taking the time to recruit, form, and nurture leadership talent.

The Roman Catholic Church has historically been a sacramental church. It offers community rites that collectively lift its peoples' eyes vertically toward God. The post-Vatican II Church has stressed that it is also a community in which people relate horizontally to each other and to the world they live in. Both the traditional and contemporary themes emphasize objective *community*. A central problem of the emergent Protestant denominations following the Reformation was that they lacked the symbols of community. They stressed the individual's nakedness before God and moral values that called for personal responsibility rather than societal responsibility.

The ethos of the United States derived largely from ascetic Protestant traditions. Liberal individualism guided the prevailing political and economic ideologies; education stressed the development of the individual; popular psychology made the feelings of the individual the measure of worth; and consumer advertising accented *me*—my gusto, my image, my consumption. American Catholics are *American,* and it is bound to show both in their most deeply held religious values and in their corporate worship. Individualism poses one of the most serious challenges to liturgical life and faith.

Our questionnaires contain an important measure of *foundational beliefs,* those beliefs and outlooks that probably are more fundamental than dogmatic symbols. This measure has several dimensions.

For some, religion is individualistic; it focuses on me and my problems. For others, religion is *communal;* it identifies the common needs of people in their social state. Religion is sometimes *vertical,* directed upward to or downward from God; at other times religion may be *horizontal,* directed outward to other people. The messages some hear in their religious values are *restricting,* while for others they may be *releasing.* Some see religion as a source of *comfort,* while others find in it a *challenge.* Individualism or social concern is identified especially in the individualistic-communal distinction.

We coded all parishioners by whether their religiosity is exclusively me-centered, whether it is exclusively social in orientation, or whether it combines the individualistic and communal themes. The paradox of American liberal individualism in a Catholic setting shows clearly in our data. Thirty-nine percent of core Catholics are individualistic; they are concerned about their own shortcomings, about how they act on God or God acts on them, and about the reward they will receive either in this life or in the afterlife. Another 18% are communal; they define the central religious problem as alienation and social disharmony, and they look for a peaceful and just social order. Twenty-one percent define their religious values through both themes, while 22% represent anomalous patterns or cannot think about religion in these terms.

It is sobering to note the dominance of individualistic themes in a Church that stresses community symbols. American individualism is a pervasive value that affects not only how people approach God, but how they deal with each other. From liturgy to politics, an individualism-preserving religion feels most comfortable with an individualism-preserving social ethic, while a community building religion seeks a community oriented social ethic.

Perhaps just as troubling as the dominance of individualistic religiosity among American core Catholics is the absence of the sacramental option from the blueprint of their foundational beliefs. Only 15% of core Catholics fit reliance on the Church's sacraments into their salvation scheme. Despite the fact that Mass attendance and communion participation are again on the upsurge, it is unclear whether the Eucharist truly has a deep meaning for Catholics.

What is clear is that Catholics, like other mainstream Americans, are more oriented in their prayer life to a Trinitarian God than to devotional pieties involving saints. The Christocentric emphasis of Vatican II is reflected in the fact that 63% of core Catholics pray to Jesus. Twenty-eight percent address God the Father, and 15% pray to the Holy Spirit. At the same time, 46% of core Catholics address prayers to Mary.

Since the same parishioner may have many objects of prayer, it is interesting to examine the extent to which Catholic prayer life is exclusively directed to the Godhead or includes prayers to the Blessed Mother and the saints. Among core Catholic parishioners, 36% of the sample address prayers exclusively to one or more members of the Trinity; 23% pray to the Trinity and the Blessed Mother; 21% pray to the Trinity, the Blessed Mother, and to saints; 7% do not pray to the Triune God, but address their prayers to Mary and various saints; and the remaining 13% have no recognizable objects of their prayer or do not pray. The Trinitarian Godhead is even more dominant in the prayer life of parish leaders: 47% pray exclusively to a member of the Godhead; 22% pray to the Trinity and the Blessed Mother; 21% pray to the Trinity, the Blessed Mother, and to saints; 7% do not pray to God, but address prayers to Mary and various saints; and only 3% have no recognizable prayer life.

In no place in our data are the differences between the devotional life of the immigrant Church and that of post-Vatican II Catholics more vividly seen than regarding the objects of prayer. For rank-and-file core Catholics under 30 years of age, 57% pray exclusively to a member of the Godhead; 25% address prayers to both the Triune God and Mary; 18% pray to the Triune God, Mary, and various saints. The figures for those between ages 30 and 40 are similar. But the Trinitarian emphasis drops precipitously among those over 40. Among the elderly, 23% are exclusively Trinitarian; 25% pray to the Triune God and Mary; 30% pray to God, Mary, and various saints; and 14% do not pray to God at all, but only address prayers to Mary and saints. Roughly 7% more of parish leaders have a Trinitarian orientation within each age group; in fact, nearly two-thirds of parish leaders under 50 pray only to members of the Godhead. Women are more likely to engage in devotions to saints than men; only one-third of core Catholic women are exclusively Trinitarian.

We are uncertain whether the emphasis on persons of the Trinity is a result of prevailing American religious values or whether it derives from Vatican II theology. The outcome is the same: the wide variety of devotional pieties found in the immigrant Church is no longer prevalent, even in the private prayer life of core Catholics. Such pieties survive mostly among older Catholics, women, and those not in the leadership ranks. Moreover, they are less often found in public worship. What visibly separated the prayer life of Catholics from that of other American Christians in times gone by is less likely to be a source of separation nowadays. In simplest man-in-the-street terms, American Protestants and Catholics may now say, "We pray to the same God."

One further feature of contemporary Catholic religiosity is found in the curious mosaic of ecumenism. Prayers to the Holy Spirit, the charismatic renewal, gospel and folk songs, neighborhood bible study—all attest the cross-fertilization of other Christian bodies with American Catholicism. Many of these cross-fertilizations have tugged Catholics in the direction of me-centered religion. Certainly the Pelagian themes of much of the folk music in our parishes derive more from the Baptist tradition than from Catholic liturgical emphases. But in the ecumenical movements, there is also a counter-thrust toward finding *community* in an objective God, in a sacramentally mediating church, and in a shared community building liturgy with responses and hymnody. The common efforts of Catholic, Lutheran, and Episcopal liturgists are instructive in this respect.

Regardless of one's taste in music, I suspect that a sense of sacramental community does not derive from me-centered words and moods. Nor does this sense just happen where liturgical planning remains uncoordinated. Those two desiderata—preparation that lets the people sense God's presence *in the community,* and coordination that shows *all* share his presence in the celebration of the community—regrettably are often lacking in our parishes. Further, data on staff and leadership indicate that the parish music leader, responsible in part for shaping the corporate worship of the community, is isolated from the parish power structure and, not infrequently, has limited contact with others who have responsibilities for preparing liturgical celebrations.

There is much we can learn from Lutheran and Episcopalian liturgical practice as to how Catholics can educate the faithful to move beyond liturgical individualism. Change can come in hymn books and service folders, in parochial schools and adult education, in the teaching objectives of the liturgist/music minister and the example of the choir member. Despite his theological individualism, Luther used hymnody and liturgical response to teach the fundamental values of a sacramental community. And absent any core collection of confessions, Anglicans carry the

entire communion—the community—in a book of common prayer and hymnody. Our 36-parish observational data show that few hymn books, psalms, or liturgical settings are in people's hands. They also show limited effort to coordinate the hymns and responses for the day with the lesson for the day. Finally, there is little evidence of the use of schools, adult education, or the liturgies themselves to instill in the people a normative tradition of liturgical life.

Lacking such normative traditions, American Catholics are faced with the deterioration of ethnic pluralism into a consensus-less liturgical individualism. Happily, some parishes in our sample shape community expression and carefully coordinate the leadership of that expression. But this is a heavy burden for the parish to bear alone. While some dioceses recognize the need to implant a normative tradition, others display too little understanding of the linkage between theology and liturgy to exercise discrimination in the selection of materials. Staff often rely on bishops for cues, and there is a short supply of trained liturgists in the bishops' ranks. Some well-meaning bishops who truly want the Church to be a participatory people of God have sanctioned liturgical materials that render it simply a collection of people.

Where do women fit into the local parish? The answer to that question is simple and straightforward: not at the top, but very close to the top. Leaving the pastor aside, women are heading the important ministries of the parish, are slightly more likely than men to be rated high in influence, and are found in visible liturgical and governance roles almost as readily as men.

Besides the decline in priestly vocations, perhaps the most consequential events in American parish life in recent decades have been the shift of women religious from traditional to nontraditional roles, and the increase of laywomen in positions of leadership. Women do not run the parish. No one would be so naive as to say that the pastor is no longer in charge; in all but about 10% of the cases, the pastor clearly is the leader of the parish team. But that team, whether formal or informal, is heavily populated by women. Further, when women religious serve on it, they often act as pastoral associates, functionally equivalent to the associate pastors in the multi-priest parishes of bygone days. Nearly one-third of all parishes have one or more women religious on the pastoral ministry staff.

Married male deacons also handle many liturgical and pastoral functions that were formerly restricted to priests. Laymen are found in the pastoral ministries of about 30% of American parishes. While we do not know the exact proportion, it appears that most of these are married laymen.

The natural inclination is to ask how these data bear on the question of the ordination of women and married men to the priesthood? We are not prepared at this point to discuss the issue in depth. We can report, however, that among our core Catholic parishioners—a sample that is slightly biased to older, female, and conservative Catholics—a substantial majority feel that married men should be allowed to become priests and a little over one-third feel that women should be allowed to become priests.

Nearly two-thirds of their parish leaders support the idea of married male priests, and a little over one-third support the ordination of women. Future analysis will reveal the kinds of Catholics who hold these positions and whether their thinking flows as a natural progression from the heavy responsibilities laypersons, especially women, have assumed for parish life. For the moment, all we have is an isolated finding that requires further examination.

PANEL DISCUSSION

FR. MURNION: Before we go on, let me say a few words about our speaker. Dr. David Leege is the director of the Center for the Study of Contemporary Society, which is in effect the applied research center for the University of Notre Dame. After completion of the first phase of the study, Dr. Leege took over the research with great interest and personal commitment. He brings to the task specific expertise in research design and measurement, having written a standard text on the subject and having served as a consultant to the National Science Foundation on the precise way to develop adequate research designs. Dr. Leege's interpretation of the early findings of the study is part of the reason why the research has received so much attention across the country.

Now, a word about our panel. We have a distinguished group of experts to help us reflect on Dr. Leege's presentation. The panelists represent different points of view on parish life in America. Our first speaker is Sr. Kathleen Hughes, a sister of the Religious of the Sacred Heart and currently associate professor of liturgy at the Catholic Theological Union here in Chicago. She also serves as an advisor to the Bishops' Committee on the Liturgy. Sr. Hughes will react to Dr. Leege's talk as one interested in the liturgical life of the parish.

SR. HUGHES: I find the results of the study fascinating. It is the sort of thing you start to read and become engaged in not just intellectually but emotionally. The strength of some of my reactions surprised me. I would like to comment as a woman religious, as a professor of liturgy, and as a member of a parish.

First, as a woman religious. Dr. Leege mentioned the serious shortage of priests. He also referred to the precipitous decline in vocations to men's and women's orders. Research shows that the limited supply of priests and sisters has certainly contributed to the changing patterns of responsibility for parish ministries. The laity have apparently stepped into the vocation gap.

I think it is really important how we interpret this information, because the interpretation will dictate the actions we take for the future. If we regard the present situation in the Church as a scarcity, a crisis, a decline, a shortage, a gap, and so on, then we will expend time, energy, and funds trying to reverse it. I cannot regard the situation in that light, nor do I think it calls for a reversal. If we really believe that the Spirit dwells in the Church, if we believe that the Spirit directs the course of the Church, then it is possible to say that we have not a decline but a true vocation explosion. Men and women, old and young, people of diverse backgrounds, professions, and education are offering to place their gifts at the service of the Church and of its ministry, either in full- or part-time service. I think that is exciting; I think it is highly significant. It suggests that now we must spend time, energy, and funds to give adequate theological and pastoral training to this cadre of ministers that has developed.

The community has come to recognize that vocation to the life of the Church and to its ministry is a right and a duty of all Catholics, by reason of their baptism. Many of those who formerly entered religious life did so because it was the only avenue to participation in the Church's ministry. That is no longer the case. Priests and religious are no longer asked, nor are they able, to care for the life of the Church alone. This, I believe, is good news. It does, however, demand some changed attitudes and a genuinely collaborative model of governance and decision making.

This leads to my first remark as a professor of liturgy. One hears that, apart from our speaking in the vernacular and the altar facing the people, some people believe Vatican II never happened. That is not all bad. I think we are overlooking the extraordinary significance of the altar facing the people. In terms of symbolic perception, it has set up the expectation among all Catholics that we will be in dialogue with one another, that we will enter into collaboration and cooperation and consultation within the community. Perhaps because we are now facing one another, we are looking, as Dr. Leege noted, for sensitivity to our needs from our priests. We are gathered around a single table as equals.

Second, there has been a dramatic increase in the number of women serving as liturgical ministers of various kinds, accompanied by a decline in those people who resist lay ministry.

A shift has occurred as to who may invade sacred space; not so long ago, the sanctuary was off limits to all but the priest and the altar boy who assisted him. This gradual change of sensibility is making it possible to imagine women as ordained leaders of the community's prayer.

I was fascinated to learn that Catholics apparently identify participation with responsorials and hymn singing. Isn't it incredible that people do not identify reception of the Eucharist as participation, despite the fact that almost everyone in the community is walking up to communion? It is clear that people attending Mass now see the Eucharist as a need. I find it peculiar that they haven't articulated this perception.

Related to the extraordinary increase in the number of people who are receiving communion is the decline in the number of people attending sacramental reconciliation. I believe that we cannot blame this decline on the reforms of Vatican II. There were studies in the late 1960s and early

1970s well before talk about the crisis of confession surfaced, showing that 75% or 80% of the Catholic population had stopped going to confession. Can we recognize in these figures that people understand other modes of sacramental reconciliation, that they experience reconciliation at many levels? Do our people so understand the reform of the rite of penance, particularly the first rite, which emphasizes a change of life and the desire to renew oneself, that they recognize they can't receive that sacrament with the same frequency? Much more study is called for before we can conclude that this decline is dire in any way. I personally believe that the reformed rite of penance is one of the best-kept secrets of the Catholic community.

I would like to comment on the decline of devotions among Catholics, particularly the young. Perhaps we must redefine what we mean by devotion and the devotional life of the community. If what we mean are rosaries, novenas, and stations of the cross, it is true they are infrequently attended. However, if the devotional life of the community is that extra-liturgical life of prayer that both leads to the celebration of the Eucharist and helps us prolong the Eucharist in our lives, then I think our devotional life is not in bad shape. The occasional Lenten vespers, the catechumenal rites, the celebration of sacramental communal reconciliation, and the scripture study which leads to solitary prayer are all strongly devotional and strongly liturgical. Such celebrations, I think, lead to a healthier Church because our extra-liturgical and liturgical lives are better integrated.

Finally, let me make a remark as a parishioner. I believe the parish community has two functions or, if you will, two constellations of functions: the nurturing function and the sending function. The parish should nurture or build up the community in faith, hope, and love in order to strengthen its members for their mission as disciples of Christ. The study suggests that the Catholic parish has been largely successful in its nurturing function, developing new models of leadership and new forms of governance, and adapting its liturgy in a way satisfactory to core parishioners. Little attention has been paid, however, to the missioning function for which nurturing exists and to which it should lead.

Perhaps this lack accounts for Dr. Leege's perception that the meaning of the Eucharist in people's lives is unclear. I regard it as a very serious failing of the liturgical reforms of parishes in general. The implications of participation in the Eucharist have not been explored. The ethical demands of participation are not clear; the relationship of liturgy to social justice remains vague; and Catholic participation in justice issues is minimal, apparently only 4% according to the data. Perhaps this is one more area that needs to be stressed as we look to the future agenda of parishes: that its sending or missioning function be regarded as equally important with its nurturing role. Then perhaps the next time parishes are studied, the people will understand what it is to which they say, "Amen" when receiving communion.

FR. MURNION: Our second respondent is Sr. Doris Gottmoeller, a member of the Sisters of Mercy. She comes to us from Cincinnati, where currently she is the provincial administrator of her order. Sr. Gottmoeller has a background in education, theology, and administration. She also combines, interestingly enough, undergraduate studies in chemistry and graduate studies in theology.

In a sense, her involvement in a national study of women in ministry involved her in examining "chemistry." The dynamics that are developing between women in ministry, on the one hand, and clergy and other men in the parish, on the other, are among the most significant in parish life today.

SR. GOTTMOELLER: I would like to begin by describing very briefly some of the findings of the Women in Ministry Study. I think there is some possibility for conversation between the two studies. Then I would like to make three or four remarks that are more eclectic and come from my life experiences.

The Women in Ministry Study is a national study of the experience of Catholic women in ministry conducted between 1977 and 1980. The principal methodology used was the telephone interview. We extensively interviewed 1,000 women. I believe they could be characterized very nicely as core Catholics with extensive parish connections, just like the women in this study. That makes a good basis for conversation between the findings of the two studies.

One thing we discovered in that study was the predominance of unpaid lay ministers. Ninety-five percent of the women interviewed were laywomen. We found this statistic startling, but I think the Notre Dame study corroborates it. The women we identified were well educated, middle class in terms of income and occupation, married, middle-aged. However, our sample did include Hispanics. We found that only 5% of the women in ministry in a national sample of 180 parishes were Hispanic, although we were careful to include a proportionate number of parishes we regarded as likely to be largely Hispanic. The number of those women in ministry was disproportionately small.

I want to say something too about the characteristics and commitment of the women we interviewed. Thirty-nine percent of them sought actively to enter ministry and 40% were recruited or elected. This forms an interesting contrast with Dr. Leege's comment that 68% of the parish ministers in the Notre Dame study were recruited.

Our evidence suggested explicit and thoughtful commitment to ministry. It was not a decision made lightly; it was not a minimal contribution; it was a deliberate and very thoughtful commitment. When asked to rate the importance of ministry in their lives on a scale of 1 to 10, 55% of the women gave it 8 or above. Ministry is a very significant feature of their lives. Eighty-six percent of the women we interviewed indicated that they expected to continue ministry indefinitely. If forced to give up ministry, the overwhelming majority, 93%, said they would be at least disturbed, while 45% would consider it a very grave loss. That reflects a very inspiring level of commitment.

Because I believe it is the prerogative of a respondent to ask questions for which she does not have any answers, I would like to raise a couple of other points and then bow gracefully from the stage. One is a perspective on parochial schools in the study, which I believe needs to be clarified. The study shows that 45% of parishes currently have schools. These schools consume probably 60% of the financial resources of their parishes.

The value and quality of the schools as educational centers have been well studied by other groups. I would challenge the sponsors of this study to explore the meaning of schools as centers of social study, bearers of Christian culture, sources of commitment and involvement for parishioners (even those who have no children in that school and are not personally involved with it), and, finally, as instruments of evangelization. I speak particularly as a member of an urban parish where the majority of the children are not Catholic. The evangelistic potential of the schools is great.

I think we need to look at the school not just as one parish program among many, but as a symbol of parish identity. The cardinal mentioned this morning that as his plane approaches O'Hare he can spot the parishes because of the schools next to them. I suggest there is a symbolism there that needs to be probed.

In May, the Ohio Catholic Conference reported in a survey of the seven dioceses in Ohio that 41% of respondents felt parishes should devote greater resources to schools. Further, 33% of the respondents felt the percentage of parish resources devoted to schools is about right. I was startled by that, and I offer it for your reflection.

Another topic is the role of women religious in the parish. This is something women religious and the present study have to examine. The research indicates that 36% of parishes today have no religious, but the converse is that 64% do. Fewer than half the parishes have schools, which indicates that religious are moving into nontraditional roles in the parishes. This is true even of parishes where there are schools. I believe this role change needs further study. The analysis should address the lack of security in generally accepted roles that women religious experience in parishes. As they look for a role in the parish, they find themselves competing with laywomen.

Again and again we encounter the unwillingness of parishes to support women religious who are no longer qualified or able to teach. When a woman has given 30 years to teaching in a classroom, often she is no longer able to continue teaching, but she can contribute 20 years or more of useful ministry. However, pastor after pastor says, "Well, it is fine if Sister wants to volunteer her services in the parish, but there is no stipend for her. We would be happy to have her in the convent if she wants to visit the sick and bring communion." The Church is very slow to find a meaningful ministry for retired sisters. That represents a great challenge.

I would suggest that we examine the attraction of religious to nonparish leadership roles. This attraction, which represents a loss to the Church, points to a real shortcoming on the part of the parish. I would want the parish to look at the value of having a stable group of full-time ministers as a model of community and center of hospitality in the parish. I believe religious themselves are not above criticism in terms of their own commitment to parish.

I will close with a comment on parishes vis-à-vis other Roman Catholic institutions. Within every diocese, existing alongside the parishes, there are Roman Catholic institutions such as high schools, colleges, hospitals, nursing homes, and child-care facilities that are also expressions of the people of God's commitment to mission. I recently asked a bishop his opinion of the high schools that the religious communities are largely supporting. He replied, "In my vision of things, those are places of temporary refuge for Catholics. The real life of the Church is in the parish." Recall that these institutions were started by religious communities at the request of the bishops and at the request of parishes. This is not the moment when the parishes and the bishops can walk away from them. There is an interdependence here that is going unrecognized.

FR. MURNION: The third respondent is Harry Fagan. Mr. Fagan was director of the Commission of Catholic Community Action in the Diocese of Cleveland. He now serves as associate director of the National Pastoral Life Center and as executive secretary of the newly formed round table for our Association of Diocesan Social Action Directors. Mr. Fagan will be responding from the viewpoint of the social ministry of the parish.

MR. FAGAN: The American parish continues to demonstrate how precariously we have wired together a hierarchical Church, attempting to use a consultative process with people who only understand democracy. I have two brief observations, one pessimistic, the other a lot more optimistic.

In reflecting on the study's findings as they relate to social ministry and the overall social mission of the Church, my pessimistic observation notes the difficulties that arise when a gospel message supporting the poor and promoting their God-given human dignity is offered to a once-immigrant, once mostly poor constituency that has become, in Dr. Leege's words, a body of parishioners who are well educated and well off financially, and who tend to be somewhat conservative. The dominance of individualistic themes in a Church that stresses community symbols could serve as an indicator of the change in Catholic thinking which was, not so long ago, more focused on the common good.

The more optimistic comment concerns Dr. Leege's observation that one of the challenges of pastoring is taking the time to recruit, form, and nurture a fresh supply of leadership talent. I suggest the issue involves a great deal more than time. The Church, our pope, and our national bishops' conference are challenging all of us to think counterculturally of racism, peace, the economy, our country's foreign policy, the death penalty, and life itself. These national and international challenges come at the same time that parishioners are hoping—to quote Dr. Leege—to have pastors that understand them and are sensitive to their needs and issues. Obviously, these different expectations cause some very real tensions, and the pastor is right in the middle, between his boss and the folks. This leads me to suggest that the issue for today's pastors is not merely taking the time but also having the skills to educate people, mediate the tensions, and reconcile the differences.

The study shows that people are, in fact, asking for more adult education. In my experience, they are also asking for more quality in that education. I think there is a great opportunity here. If priests are to grasp this opportunity, the focus of their own formation programs must change. No longer is it sufficient to emphasize the pastor's spirituality, his relationship with his bishop, his fraternity with other priests, and his psychological needs. In the face of very natural tensions centering around the social mission of the Church, there is a real need for priests to develop skills related to convening adult education sessions, listening, conflict management, time management, project management, delegation, and, in general, helping the laity become involved in social ministry. There is still not a seminary in the country that teaches conflict management.

FR. MURNION: Our final respondent is one of those pastors caught in the middle, Fr. Brian Joyce. He comes from the Diocese of Oakland, where he has served as adult education director and chancellor. For the past six years, Fr. Joyce has been pastor of St. Monica's Parish. He has also been a member of the Bishops' Committee on Priestly Life and Ministry. Fr. Joyce, a frequent retreat master for priests, is also involved in training programs for priests and was instrumental in developing a training program for new pastors in California. He will respond to Dr. Leege's talk from the viewpoint of the ministry of pastors.

FR. JOYCE: I find Dr. Leege's paper heartening. It is heartening in terms of the way renewal is going. My own experience corroborates the study's findings. In our parish we have about 750 adults at church each weekend and close to 700 who are in stable ongoing ministries in the parish, related either to governance or social action. I wonder, however, whether this trend will last and grow. Will it lead to a deeper social concern as part of the mission of the parish? It seems to me the deciding factor is going to be effective leadership. I don't want to limit effective leadership just to ordained priests or the pastor, and yet their leadership roles need to be addressed.

I realize that it is theology and opportunity that allow participation to grow in our parishes, but this participation is mediated through people. For better and for worse, today it is mediated primarily through pastors, and I think we have a crisis among our parish priests. They face greatly heightened expectations and demands. We have 63 language groups in

California and that affects almost every parish and parish priest today. Priests are fewer and older. I am part of an endangered species and that gets mixed reviews. One of the reasons reviews are mixed is that there is a very thin line between being a pivotal person and being a bottleneck.

How do you deal with this crisis of leadership? Let me suggest five or six possibilities. For one thing, provision should be made for personal affirmation of parish priests. I know from working with people that there is no growth where there is no affirmation. Along with affirmation, we have to redevelop a fairly strong presbyteral identity. I can remember—I am ordained long enough—going to a priests' retreat where I knew most or at least some of the other men. I don't think that is common anymore. We don't have common retreats; we come from different cultures and different languages; we come from different seminaries and different ecclesiologies. The one hopeful thing I see around the country is development of presbyteral convocations, so for the first time in an individual diocese, some of the priests actually see each other and get a sense of who they are. I think that is a building block for leadership in the future.

Third, I would like to see the development of collaborative skills. I think this is the kind of thing that Harry Fagan was referring to. I would add that our continuing education should be collaborative. If I go to a continuing education workshop as the pastor of my parish to learn how to work with my parish staff, my parish staff had better be there, and they had better be with me when I go home. We must develop models where priests do not attend clergy education classes just with other priests or just with laypeople and staff from other parishes.

I think we need standards for parish life. Presently, it is up to the whim of the pastor whether a parish has an RCIA program, a parish council, or anything else. That worked pretty well with the old Polish pastor who was in a parish for 55 years. But now pastors are changing every six years, every five years, every three years, and whole efforts at renewal are being dismantled overnight. I don't know how much instability parishes and parish staffs can take.

Developing such standards will not be easy, but I remain hopeful. With them must come personnel procedures that are both derivative from and supportive of the standards. At present, if a pastor is to be transferred, we examine a profile of the parish, its needs and style, and then we look at who is available to succeed him. Sometimes there are few men available. It comes down to a choice between supporting what is going on in the life of that parish and deciding on the basis of seniority or clericalism or the desire to avoid confrontation. Often enough, the choice goes against the standards in the parish and against parish life. I think this needs attention.

I think we have to communicate. The Vatican should realize that renewal is working in the United States, that people are going to church. Somehow, I don't think that message is clear. We have to communicate in the other direction, too, through adult education. I am pleased that the study reveals interest in education. Still, the response is not as enthusiastic as might be hoped for; we have to pay more than lip service to adult education.

FR. MURNION: I am sure Dr. Leege would like to respond to the panelists. Let us take a few moments, though, to entertain questions, comments, and alternative views from the audience.

PARTICIPANT: My name is Jim Jennings from the Campaign for Human Development. I just want to second what several of the panelists said regarding the future direction of Dr. Leege's studies. In some ways, we have a white, successful, powerful, pragmatic, well-educated, middle-class Church. But, there are also vast numbers of other people who are not in that category at all. Given the preferential option for the poor, there is a great need for the Church to respond to this reality. This seems to me crucial to the study of parish.

PARTICIPANT: I am Bill McCready from the National Opinion Research Center. I would like to raise a question about the definition of "core Catholic" and its implications for ecclesiology. It seems to me if you define as "core Catholic" older, conservative women, you have a problem. Younger people and Hispanics, but younger people especially, are very badly represented in this study. They are not the younger people that are in the parishes. How useful, then, are the data as a beacon? How useful is it to help us look into the future when the difference between the young people in this study and the young people in other studies, in terms of church attendance and other measures, is so dramatic? Why not choose a phrase like "traditional Catholic" instead of "core Catholic"? "Core" implies centrality, importance, superiority; I think we ought to grapple with that.

FR. MURNION: The quick answer to your question is that we studied registered parishioners. They might or might not be traditional. The basis on which they could be part of the sample was simply registration.

PARTICIPANT: I am Fr. Bob Pelton from Notre Dame. This is a comment on the strong individualism that presently appears among Roman Catholics in our country. A greater awareness of the Hispanic presence in the Church might lead to greater sensitivity to the communitarian dimension. The base communities in Latin America point very clearly in that direction. Researchers should bear this in mind as they move into the study of Hispanics in the United States.

FR. MURNION: Now I'll invite Dr. Leege to respond to some of the questions and comments he has heard.

DR. LEEGE: I think the most difficult problem we faced in the design of the survey was deciding what a Catholic is and what kind of Catholics we were going to reach by this kind of a research design. The problem with using some term other than "core Catholic" is that other terms don't fit very well either. "Traditional Catholic" doesn't fit. We have many people in our samples who do not practice the kinds of devotions, frequent confession, fasting, and so forth that characterize traditional Catholics. It is too representative a sample to be captured by the term "traditional Catholic." We can't call it a sample of older Catholics because a very substantial proportion of young people are included. We can, however, identify the sample's bias in terms of participation in central rites. We know it is about 20% more participatory in central rites than a comparable General Social Survey sample. I would welcome an alternative to "core Catholic," but I don't think "nuclear" or "traditional" is appropriate.

With regard to individualism and missioning, we are starting to prepare some data about people's perceptions of what a parish is supposed to be. These data will reveal something about individualism and sense of mission. We will be able to capture the extent to which people see the parish as a retreat, a solace, a balm for woes; the extent to which it builds a sense of family and community; the extent to which it releases and motivates people to move out on some sort of mission. We will also examine the priorities people set for their parishes, the kinds of activities they feel their parishes should engage in.

THE AMERICAN CATHOLIC PARISH A HISTORICAL PERSPECTIVE 1820–1980

SPEAKER

Dr. Jay P. Dolan
Associate Professor of History, University of Notre Dame
Director, Cushwa Center for the Study of American Catholicism

MODERATOR

Dr. Francis J. Butler
President, FADICA

INTRODUCTION: A VARIETY OF PARISH PASTS

Every social institution has a history. The parish is no exception. Under the guidance of the spirit of God, each parish is today also the result of many social forces, stimulating and nourishing each other. To understand parishes we cannot simply take a slice of current time. Memory is short. There is a tendency to recall the past selectively so that it is consistent with the present. Thus, the methods of both sociology and history must be merged to understand American Catholic parishes twenty years after Vatican II.

Parishes are products of the larger society in which they are embedded. An ecclesiastical history that focuses on church leaders, while valuable, takes us only part way in the understanding of parishes. We must write history from the bottom up as well as from the top down. We look at American parishes partly as the product of internal church forces, but heavily as the product of broader social forces operating throughout American history.

A major component of the Notre Dame Study of Catholic Parish Life was the writing of a history of the parish. This history had a special twist. It was divided geographically into six different regions of the country. Each region was assigned its own historian who would research and write the history of the development of the parish within that geographic region. The benefit of such an approach is the ability to *compare* the development of the parish in different geographical regions of the U.S. Such comparisons were made possible because each historian followed the same thematic outline in writing his or her regional history. They studied parish locales, size, ethnicity, role of laity, clerical leadership, organizational complexity, popular pieties, religious socialization and education, and ecumenism.

History continually reminds us of the reality of change in our lives and in our cultures. The historical study of Catholic parishes teaches us the same lesson. In the United States there has never been one typical parish that has dominated the landscape during the course of the last 200 years. St. Peter's parish in New York City, founded in 1785, has served a variety of communities throughout its two-hundred-year history; though the building has stood on the same spot for nearly two centuries, the nature and style of parish life has changed with the changing times. The same is true of Indian mission churches in New Mexico, Arizona, and California. Founded in the eighteenth century, many of these mission communities are still functioning but the parishioners have changed and so too have their respective environments.

In the early nineteenth century a distinctive type of parish did exist in the Northeastern United States where the bulk of Americans and Catholics lived. Since in many instances the people had preceded the priest, leadership in the parish initially fell upon the shoulders of laymen. Once the priest arrived, people and priest had to learn to work together for the benefit of all. A system of governance, common in American Protestant churches and in some European countries, was worked out whereby laymen, elected by the people, worked with the priest in managing the affairs of the parish. Called trustees, these laymen were the recognized leaders in the parish and had a very strong voice in church affairs. History has not been kind to this tradition in American Catholicism and has wrongly depicted the trustee system and lay trustees as detrimental to Catholic life. Though the system certainly had some problems because of irascible laymen and authoritarian priests, it worked remarkably well in numerous parish communities where, in the words of Bishop John England of Charleston, South Carolina, "The laity are empowered to cooperate but not to dominate." In a sense, the post-Vatican II American Church is now returning to its lay roots.

The early nineteenth-century parish also had a distinctive style of liturgy or worship. In these early years the liturgy was noted for its plainness. The interior of churches was spartan with few, if any, of the decorative statues or paintings that were so common in European churches. The practice of religion centered around Sunday, with the celebration of morning Mass, afternoon vespers and benediction comprising the core of Catholic devotional life. During this era religious education took place in an informal manner with the home being the principal setting; only a few urban parishes were able to establish a school.

By 1900 the Catholic parish had changed dramatically. In the intervening years millions of Catholic immigrants from Ireland, Germany, Italy, Poland, and other Eastern European countries had arrived in the United States. Attracted to this country by an expanding economy, they provided the muscle that enabled industrial America to prosper. By 1900 the Church in the United States had become a church of the immigrants; it was a blue-collar church centered in the working class neighborhoods of urban America. More than 70% of the United States population lived in the economic heartland of the nation, a region that stretched from the Atlantic Seaboard to the Mississippi River and was bordered on the south by the Ohio River Valley. The Southeast was still missionary country as were parts of the rural West.

In the immigrant neighborhoods the parish was a central community institution. Most often organized according to language or nationality, it gave the newcomers a sense of identity in a strange new world. Since the people generally arrived before the priest, they took an active role in the initial stages of organizing the parish. Most groups adopted some form of trustee government, but the clergy and hierarchy did not look kindly on such lay involvement in the governance of the local Church. As the numbers of clergy increased and the institutional Church became better organized with the establishment of numerous dioceses, bishops and pastors assumed control of the local Church and the laity were left to "pay, pray, and obey," as one pundit put it. With the demise of lay leadership in the parish, the focal point of the people's involvement shifted especially to the devotional arena but also to the benevolence societies.

Throughout the Catholic world a devotional revolution had taken place by the second half of the nineteenth century. Promoted by the papacy and the hierarchy, it was received with enthusiasm by most of the American Catholic community. Gone was the plainness of the early nineteenth century and in its place was an elaborate network of devotions, both public and private; churches were decorated with numerous statues and paintings depicting favorite local saints; travelling revivalists or mission preachers promoted this devotional Catholicism; and parish confraternities, organized around a particular devotion, sustained the people's interest. Some immigrant groups promoted their own unique traditions, like the Italian *festa* and the Mexican passion play.

Devotional Catholicism and the devotional parish were central ingredients in defining American Catholic identity at the neighborhood level. Another key element in defining this identity was the parochial school. Born in the midst of large-scale immigration and at a time when the public schools were still Protestant institutions, the parochial school had become widely accepted by the end of the nineteenth century; about 40% of the parishes had such a school at that time. A major reason for the extraordinary growth of the Catholic school was the availability of a large pool of teachers who were willing to work at less than subsistence wages; these were, of course, the women religious, who along with a much smaller number of religious brothers, comprised the teaching staff of the Catholic schools. To illustrate the commitment of the parish to the school, Joseph Casino examined parish financial records in the Northeast and discovered that in 1900 as much as 50% of the entire parish budget went to support the parish school. Parishes in other regions of the country made similar financial commitments to the school.

At this time the parish school was the primary religious educator in the Catholic community; for those children who did not attend parochial schools—and that represented well over half the school-age population—the home and the family remained the primary religious educator. In that day and age catechism classes were neither well organized nor terribly effective.

TRANSITION INTO THE MIDDLE OF THE TWENTIETH CENTURY

During the first half of the twentieth century little change took place in the parish in terms of leadership, liturgy, and religious education. The pastor was still very much a reigning monarch and longer tenures for pastors tended to strengthen their position. Devotional Catholicism flourished, as novenas and missions became the most popular expressions of the people's piety. Parochial schools increased in number and, though they never reached more than half of the school-age Catholic population, they still remained one of the distinctive features of the immigrant Church into the first half of the twentieth century. In the Southeast the Catholic Church was beginning to develop a more visible presence; the same was evident in the Far West. It was a boom time for American Catholicism as new parish churches, schools, and other institutions began to rise up across the landscape. Such extensive building taxed the financial resources of most parishes and huge debts became standard. To raise more money the Sunday envelope system was introduced and bazaars, raffles, and other fund-raising events became an integral part of parish life. Benevolence societies, such as St. Vincent de Paul, continued to deal with the problems of the less fortunate.

Major social changes took place during these decades and they were destined to change decisively the American Catholic landscape. One major change was the end of immigration from Europe; new laws passed by Congress in the 1920s stopped the flow of immigration and, for the first time in over a century, European immigrants would no longer dominate the agenda of the Church. Nonetheless, a new immigration developed north from Mexico and this flow of immigrants would soon pose serious challenges for the local Church. Another equally important challenge was the migration north of numerous black Americans. As these new immigrants settled in the inner cities where the old immigrants lived, the city began to expand outward to the crabgrass frontier of the suburb. Many Catholics followed this movement to the suburbs and new parishes began to spring up in these areas.

By the 1940s it was clear that, as a group, Catholics were becoming more middle class and increasingly more American and less European; this pattern of development was truer of the older immigrant groups like the Germans and the Irish than it was of the more recent arrivals like the Italians and the Polish.

Another change that would have a profound effect on the future of Catholicism was an awakening within the community of a concern for justice. This concern first surfaced in late nineteenth-century America but never pervaded the Catholic community to any significant degree; the depression of the 1930s and the social encyclicals of the popes changed that. Both clergy and laypeople became intensely interested in issues of social justice and, though this movement was independent of the local parish, the effects of this new consciousness would eventually leave their mark on the parish. In addition to the concern for justice came a new theology of the Church; called the theology of the mystical body, it inspired many laypeople to become more committed to the mission of the Church in the world.

These changes, both social and theological, were for the most part glacial movements whose effects would not be widely felt for some time. While these changes were occurring, the parish remained intact and seemingly immune to change. Joseph Fichter's study of a southern parish in the late 1940s revealed a parish that was in many respects not very different from its 1900s predecessor.

THE CONTEMPORARY PARISH

The parish of the 1980s, however, is quite different from its early nineteenth-century predecessor as well as its 1900s counterpart. The Catholic population has changed significantly in the last quarter century. Catholics resemble the rest of the American population in terms of birthplace, class, and education; though the majority of them still live in the economic heartland of the nation, that region that stretches from the Atlantic Coast to the Mississippi north of the Ohio River Valley, many now live in the suburbs rather than the nation's central cities. This means that the suburban parish is replacing the urban neighborhood parish as the normative experience for a plurality of Catholics. Gone is the public nature of city neighborhood living and in its place is the more privatized life style of the suburb. Left behind in this move to the new world of the suburb were many of the traditions of immigrant, folk Catholicism.

The newest immigrants, the vast majority of whom are Spanish-speaking newcomers from Mexico and other Latin American countries, reside in the nation's central cities, often in the same buildings once inhabited by Italian, Polish, Irish, and Slovak Catholics. Their numbers have increased so greatly in the last twenty-five years that in many areas of the country—Florida and California being two good examples—they comprise better than half of the Catholic population. In the Far West immigrants from Asian countries give the Church a decidedly Oriental cast. The large numbers of new Catholic immigrants from Asia and Latin America have once again given the Church in America a pronounced multicultural quality. But instead of being multicultural European, the Church in America is becoming multicultural in a global manner.

In the nineteenth century the mainstream of American Catholicism was made up of foreign-born immigrants; along the margins of the community was a small but powerful middle class. Today the mainstream is comprised of middle-class Catholics who are culturally very American; from this group come the decision makers and the power brokers. On the margin of the community in terms of influence are the new immigrants who, as has been noted, make up the majority of the Catholic population in some regions. It is not unlike the situation in the nineteenth century when the Irish, for a variety of reasons, dominated the seats of power in the Church and lorded it over other immigrant groups who, in many communities, outnumbered the people from Erin. The scars this left among immigrant communities are still visible today. How the contemporary situation is resolved in terms of meeting the cultural needs of the new immigrants is a critical question that today's Catholic leadership must face.

Of course another major influence on the parish of the 1980s was the Second Vatican Council. Its articulation of a new theology of the Church, of a new understanding of the use of authority in the Church, and the sponsorship of a new liturgy have had a tremendous impact on parish life in the last quarter century.

The social revolutions of post-World War II America also placed a heavy burden on the parish. The linking of better education to better job opportunities, the civil rights movement, the Vietnam War, the nuclear arms race, the peace movement, instantaneous telecommunications that bring the plight of the underdeveloped world into our living rooms, new employment opportunities outside the home and increased educational opportunities for women, policy dissatisfaction and the questioning of traditional authority—all had an impact on Catholic Americans. For many younger Catholics, their hopes and dreams were uplifted by a young Catholic president, but expectations unmet only led to further disillusionment with the upheavals of the 1960s and the malaise of the 1970s. At precisely that time in American history, the Catholic Church was trying to welcome reform, to sift the good from the bad.

Given the scope of the social and religious changes of the last quarter century, it is not surprising to discover that the parish of the 1980s differs from its predecessors. One area of comparison is parish leadership. For a number of reasons, both theological and sociological, laypeople are much more involved in parish decision making. A common form of this participation is through the parish council. Such lay participation is quite different from the early twentieth century when the clergy still acted alone. Nonetheless, not all parishes have adopted this type of church government; in Florida, for example, only about one-third of the parishes in the Miami archdiocese have a parish council. By contrast, every parish in the Savannah, Georgia diocese has a parish council, according to Michael McNally. Of course, having a parish council does not mean that democracy reigns in the Catholic Church in America. Far from it. Nevertheless, this is a very important development in parish life. In some areas of the country this development is especially important because of the large number of parish communities without a priest in residence; such is the case in many locales of the Rocky Mountains and inter-mountain regions.

Of course there are other areas of parish life where leadership styles have changed dramatically since 1900. One that quickly comes to mind is the liturgy. Many parishes have formed liturgical committees made up of priests, women religious and laypeople; rather than just one person— the priest—being responsible for the liturgy, a group of people now take an active role in planning parish liturgies. The same development has taken place in the areas of religious education, youth work, and financial affairs; the ubiquitous committee form of decision making has replaced the one-person rule of days past. In fact, parish consultation has become a cottage industry in the American Catholic community. Even though laypeople may not have the impact they seek through parish councils, they have discovered that by *doing* the many ministries of the parish, they can have a pervasive effect on the life of the parish.

Just as the style of leadership has changed, so too, have the patterns of piety. What Flannery O'Connor called the "novena-rosary" style of religion has undergone a dramatic decline. Gone is the elaborate network of devotional Catholicism with its statues, medals, scapulars, novenas, and parish revivals, and in its place have come biblically oriented meditation booklets, public penitential services, prayer groups and parish mission statements. Undoubtedly the most visible indicator of this change in Catholics' devotional or spiritual lives is the variety of Sunday liturgies or Masses in the parish. The longing for order, so central a feature of the Church in the immigrant era, has given way to a longing for pluralism, not just in theology but in popular piety as well. In days past different styles of piety were associated with different immigrant groups; a trip inside a Polish church left a decidedly different impression than a visit to a church in an Irish neighborhood. Today within the same parish community, a visitor can observe quite different styles of liturgies that are indicative of very diverse patterns of piety. The 8:00 A.M. Mass is often strikingly different from the 10:30 A.M. Mass; it is almost as though there are different congregations within the same parish.

One of the most dramatic changes in Catholic piety is the popularity of charismatic religion. The charismatic movement swept through the Church in the 1970s and has revitalized the religion of thousands of American Catholics. Today, Catholic charismatics have become an integral part of many parish communities and their style of piety has won acceptance from other Catholics after a long period of suspicion. Spiritual renewal, whether charismatic or not, is indeed a powerful force in parishes. For individuals it may come from Cursillo weekends; for entire parishes it may result, for example, from the RENEW program. Marriage Encounter may not only enrich a marriage but lead a couple to see God in a new light. Many parishes attribute their new sense of purpose and vitality to these openings to the Holy Spirit.

No one needs to be told about the decline in the number of Catholic schools. This has been trumpeted for several years. But how great has this decline been? One way of answering this question is to look at statistics from specific regions; what emerges is quite striking. Put simply, in most areas of the country, there were more parochial schools in operation in 1930 than in 1980. In Oregon, for example, 54 Catholic parochial schools were operating in 1930; in 1980 the number was 51; in Massachusetts the 1930 figure was 275 and the 1980 number was 218. In other words, after 50 years of substantial growth in the young Catholic population, the number of Catholic schools in some regions has actually declined. In the intervening years there *was* a large expansion in the number of schools but then came the subsequent contraction of the past two decades. This decline is most visible in the suburbs, where many parishes have chosen not to invest in schools.

Comparing the number of clergy and the number of women religious in 1930 in some regions with 1980 figures reveals similar results; the number of Catholics has increased but the number of church personnel is not much different from 50 years ago. Such comparisons suggest that nowadays American Catholicism is less institutionally developed than it was 50 years ago. The implications of this remain to be seen, but it is no coincidence that dioceses now devote substantial staff resources to workshops and training programs for the laity.

The decline in Catholic schools has changed the thrust of religious education in the parish. In an unprecedented manner adult education has moved to the forefront of the parochial educational commitment, and in any given season, most Catholic parishes offer a variety of religious education programs for adults. More so than in the immigrant Church, the family has become involved in the religious education of children, even in parishes that still have a parochial school. Because of the decline in the number of women religious, more laypeople are becoming involved in the teaching apostolate both as volunteers and as paid personnel. The Confraternity of Christian Doctrine (CCD) is a major avenue for teaching ministry, especially among mothers in the parish.

The changes in parish life are obvious to any middle-aged Catholic—Mass in English; laypeople reading the Scriptures at Mass; women religious working in the parish not as parochial school teachers but as pastoral associates, directors of religious education or social action programs; popular election of parish councils; and laypeople distributing the Eucharist. It is equally obvious that not all parishes have changed with the same measure of conviction; in fact many have resisted the movement for change in the areas of leadership, liturgy, and education. Some parishes are like volleyballs; diocesan assignment of a new pastor leads to the dismantling of liturgical or programmatic changes just as the parish is finally adjusting to those changes introduced by the previous pastor four years earlier. Now that lay volunteers are deeply involved in parish liturgies and ministries, the laity is especially sensitive to the directions a parish takes as the result of a bishop's assignment of priests. Whatever the outcomes, it is clear that the parish of the future will more resemble the parish of the 1980s than its counterpart in the 1940s and 1950s. The reason for this is plain.

The forces of change are too powerful and too deeply rooted to be ignored or sidestepped. The Catholic parish of the nineteenth century could not resist adapting to the social forces of immigration and urbanization; if it did it would have become an anachronism. Nor could it resist the devotional revolution that swept through the Roman Catholic world. Today much the same is true. The social implications of suburbanization are too widespread and too powerful to ignore; as a group, Catholics are economically better off today than they were 50 years ago; they are better educated and consequently expect more from their local Church; women religious are better educated and seek more challenges in a variety of ministries; the education and professionalization of laywomen has freed a powerful force in the local Church; and the demands and needs of the new immigrants are different from mainstream Catholics. To be a living force in society the Church will have to adapt itself to this changing social environment.

There have also been changes in the deepest religious values. Once the Second Vatican Council sanctified the principle of participation of the people in the liturgy, the celebrations of Mass and the sacraments were destined to change. The moment the Council defined the Church as the people of God, a change in thinking took place and eventually a change in acting as well; the concept of shared responsibility entered into church life and with it came shared decision making. These changes have been developing for close to 20 years and in ways most likely not envisioned by the bishops at the Council. History is like that. No one can predict the future, but release a powerful agent for change in a society undergoing rapid transformation and the future is unlikely to imitate the past.

FLOOR DISCUSSION

DR. BUTLER: Our expert on the history of the parish has been Dr. Jay Dolan, director of the Historical Research Section of the parish study. Dr. Dolan, a graduate of the University of Chicago, is also associate professor in Notre Dame's Department of History and director of the Cushwa Center for the Study of American Catholicism. He is the author of several books on the Catholic parish, including *The Immigrant Church: New York's Irish and German Catholics, 1815–1865* and *Catholic Revivalism: The American Experience, 1830–1900*. This fall will see the publication of yet another book entitled *American Catholicism: A Social History from Colonial Times to the Present*.

Perhaps we can devote a few minutes now to questions and comments from the audience on Dr. Dolan's presentation.

PARTICIPANT: Why was a regional approach taken to the history of the parish? I would think there is as much diversity in each region as similarity. Perhaps it would have been better to write a history of the rural, the urban, and the suburban parish, tracing common elements in different parts of the country.

DR. DOLAN: Fr. Murnion and I decided on this approach after considerable discussion. For one thing, it allows the writer to develop the story of a particular region centered on the parish as an institution. Second, I think one value of the Notre Dame study is that it highlights the uniqueness of each region.

Reading the history of the development of the parish in the West taught me many valuable things I did not know. For example, the religious orders were used much like the Marines. They would come into places in Montana, Utah, Nevada, and they would establish the beachhead, planting the Catholic community in that particular area. Then, once the parish got established and there was a Catholic presence, the orders left town and the regular diocesan clergy came in and began to foster parish life. We all think about religious orders in terms of hospital work and schools. But they played a very important role in the development of the parish in many frontier areas in the late nineteenth and early twentieth centuries.

The regional approach also allows you to compare region with region. If you did the suburban parish, the urban parish, the rural parish, the black parish, the Hispanic parish, I think you would lose some of the breadth that we have achieved through these six different histories. Comparative developments in the South and in the West are interesting. While ours is not the only legitimate path to take, I think it proved to be valuable.

PARTICIPANT: The regional approach might be less valid in the contemporary situation because of the considerable homogenization that better communications has brought about. For earlier periods, however, the regional approach would be essential in light of the profound differences by region caused by the pattern of immigration and a number of other factors.

DR. DOLAN: It also enabled us to fill in some very big holes in Catholic historiography, especially as regards the South and Southwest.

PARTICIPANT: What were the major elements in the transition from the period of lay leadership to the more clerically oriented period? Are there any key factors that should be singled out?

DR. DOLAN: One factor was obviously the presence of more clergy. In the early period when the parish was just developing, there were marriages, baptisms, and funerals without benefit of clergy. Then as the Church became more institutionalized and more personnel became available, the potential emerged for more clerical leadership.

Also very important was the ecclesiology that developed in the nineteenth century during the reign of Pius IX. It is a more monarchical view of the Church, where the power flows downward from the pope to the bishop to the pastor, and the people are left to pray, pay, and obey.

The desire for unity played a part. There were 28 different language groups in the immigrant Church in America. In some places in Chicago, priests actually walked around with a pistol in their belt because there was so much interparish hostility. That is a fact. Clerical leadership provided the control to unify these different groups.

PARTICIPANT: Could you comment on the role of service in these various periods?

DR. DOLAN: I think it is fair to say that in the first period service was what the family rendered to its own. During the second period you get into the traditional Catholic works of charity: hospitals caring for the sick, youth organizations, and so on.

The parish itself was not capable of serving a very large constituency because of its resources, both human and financial. The major parish organizations were the St. Vincent de Paul Society and maybe some women's charitable organizations that did work for people in the parish, much as they do today. The larger apostolates were located beyond the parish, in the hospitals, the settlement houses. Even today the parish is not very oriented toward social action; it is very oriented toward traditional services like charitable works.

The concept of participation is very important. People argue that today the laity are participating much more in parish life. I don't think that is true. I think that in 1890 people participated as much as they do today, but they participated differently. Today they are doing things no one dreamed of a hundred years ago. In 1890, the sanctuary was a sacred place, the realm of the priest. Today there is a sense of informality; laypeople *are* participating in the liturgy. I would argue that there was as much lay involvement then in devotional societies as there is in parish affairs in 1980. But today, because of a different ecclesiology and a different concept of ministry, laypeople are participating differently.

PARTICIPANT: My name is Donald Gallagher, from the DeRance Foundation. How predominant do you find the voluntary element in modern parish life? Do many people still follow the traditional practice of attending the parish in their own neighborhood? Also, to what extent does church authority approve voluntary affiliation? Will the pattern continue, perhaps transforming the parish from a territorial entity to a professional group or workers' group or something of that sort?

DR. DOLAN: The Notre Dame study found that the incidence of people picking out their own parish is not very high. Few people are choosing a parish as one chooses a barber or something like that.

On the other hand, the concept of the voluntary parish seems to be taking hold. Many people are particular about their religion and are particular about what parish they attend. Just because they live on a certain street does not mean they are going to go to the parish covering that territory. This trend, I think, will become more noticeable. Already, some parishes are trying to market themselves, creating, for example, a better liturgy to attract people. Whether the voluntary parish will become dominant, however, I cannot say.

PARTICIPANT: I am Peter Robinson from Brencanda. What lessons, in your opinion, do the experiments in lay trusteeism hold for us today? Do you think history demonstrates that clerical domination is a function of the number of clergy available?

DR. DOLAN: No. I think the lesson of the period of lay trusteeism is that clergy and laypeople have to learn how to work together and to get along together. They have to learn how to cooperate and not dominate. In the nineteenth century one of the key reasons for clerical dominance, in my opinion, was not numbers but ecclesiology. The operative view of the Church, the nature of the Church, was such that the clergy was in control.

Pius X used the analogy of the shepherd and his flock. The bishop was the shepherd; the people were the sheep and they followed the shepherd. There are new images today and a new style of leadership.

PARTICIPANT: I am Fr. Tom Ventura. Some of our people who work with vocational recruitment suggest that we have two church populations coexisting side by side, at least in an urban area like Chicago. There is one kind of vocation that traditionally goes through the minor seminary, the college seminary, the major seminary; this is associated with what we call the immigrant type of Catholic: Puerto Ricans, Mexicans, blacks, Polish, Eastern Europeans who have come to this country relatively late. Side by side with that is a post-immigrant Catholicism, which produces later vocations, people who have gone through high school, college, and perhaps have even gone into the workplace and will come into the seminary at the age of 23, 24, or 26. One of the challenges I see today is to learn to live with both these populations. Would you comment?

DR. DOLAN: I think one of the most important modern developments is the phenomenon of the new immigrants. To most white middle-class Catholics, the influx of immigrants is something that happened in the past. But there is a tremendous flow of new immigrants coming into this country every year. We lose sight of that. I think it is terribly important to realize that the immigrant Church is still with us. That is a basic pastoral reality.

Then you have the other church, the American Church, the church of the immigrants which has become more and more American and is an entirely changed entity.

I think the distinction you are making is fundamental. However, I am not in a position to relate it to the vocation situation.

PARTICIPANT: Ethnicity was very strong in the Church in the nineteenth century. Is ethnicity a thing of the past or is it just coming into its own because of the new immigrants?

DR. DOLAN: I think you have to work with the new immigrants, many of whom are Catholic, just as you worked with the old immigrants. That is a personal belief. I think the national parish, the ethnic parish, is still a viable institution. Ethnicity remains strong in the new groups. They just arrived and they need a period of adjustment; they need different pastoral care than the people in the suburbs.

PARTICIPANT: But even with the Irish, the Poles, and the Germans, ethnic differences are not altogether gone. They remain a powerful factor in the Church in America. Many studies show that you have to deal with ethnic family systems differently in order to avoid real problems.

DR. DOLAN: I agree, but there is a distinction to be made. The powerful strain of ethnicity appears predominately with more recent immigrants. By that I mean not only the Hispanics and Asians who are currently entering the country but also the late-nineteenth, early twentieth-century Italians and Poles. While the Irish and Germans may retain some ethnic traces, for the most part they have become Americanized. Different immigrant groups display different tendencies, different likes and dislikes, different personalities, different styles. So from the Church's point of view there are layers upon layers. No one pastoral strategy is going to work for all these layers.

PASTORS: CHALLENGES AND EXPECTATIONS IN A TIME OF CHANGE

SPEAKER

Fr. Thomas F. Ventura
Vicar for Priests, Archdiocese of Chicago

Pastors in our diocese describe themselves as being at the bottom of a huge funnel. Everyone in the Church—the pope, the cardinal, the national Catholic offices in Washington, the chancery office, the diocesan agencies—all pour their pet projects, programs, suggestions, or directives into the pastor's funnel. Parishioners and local organizations also join in. The president of the parish council, the school principal, the scout leader, the janitor, the pro-life coordinator, the school board president drop notes, letters, memos, and complaints into the funnel and they end up each day on the desk of the pastor.

How does he deal with the load? While each pastor has his own style, the things that come through the funnel seem to get divided into three categories. First, there are the items that go into the wastebasket. Then there are the items that go into a large stack of papers on his desk—matters he will get to later. Finally, there are those relatively few high-priority items that receive immediate attention. (Something is more likely to get into category three if the pastor will encounter the sender personally within the next week.)

The funnel theory underscores the importance of the parish, the fundamental unit in the Church. The pastor is the pivotal person in the parish. The funnel theory is also behind my remarks today. About a year ago, I circulated a simple questionnaire developed by Msgr. Colin MacDonald and the NCCB Committee on Priestly Life and Ministry. The response was impressive. Pastors were able to pour their concerns, hopes, hurts, complaints, joys, insights into the funnel that empties onto *my* desk. The survey was an important element in a convergence of concerns about pastors and parishes. It has had a ripple effect. Since then, several things have happened in our archdiocese:

1. Two overnight meetings were conducted by pastors for pastors on the subject of "Effective Pastoring in a Transitional Church." About 50 pastors attended each session.

2. A five-day retreat was conducted by pastors for pastors. Forty-five pastors attended, including Cardinal Bernardin.

3. The Association of Chicago Priests sponsored a two-day workshop on "Collaboration between Men and Women in Parish Ministry" that was attended by 20 priests and 20 women staff members.

4. There has been growing interest in and discussion of the newly developing position of parish business manager. A number of parishes already have such a person on their staff. We are beginning to discuss ways in which inner-city parishes might share a business manager and how they might get help to pay the salary.

5. We have begun a training program for new pastors. They attend four sessions during their first year in the job. Each five-hour meeting focuses on one key aspect of parish life: the head (religious education from the cradle to the grave); the heart (liturgy, prayer, spiritual growth); the hand (Christian service, care of the sick, outreach, social justice); and the nitty-gritty (finances, building management, personnel issues, staff development). Thus far, 20 new pastors have attended each of the first

two sessions. We also have a system of mentoring by which experienced pastors assist those just starting out.

6. The 1990 Project has surveyed 23 representative parishes about their preparations for a future in which there will be more Catholics to serve and fewer priests. One finding is that lay leaders strongly encourage the Church to ordain married men and women, if necessary, so that we have enough ordained ministers.

7. Lewis College in Lockport, Illinois, has initiated a series of seminars in their business school to help pastors develop additional skills.

8. The Association of Chicago Priests sponsored a "Creative Pastoring Day" attended by approximately 250 parish ministers. It focused on responsible uses of the theological principle of *Epekia* (or legitimate exceptions to the law) in dealing with such sensitive pastoral issues as divorce and remarriage, the sacrament of reconciliation, and women's role in the Church.

All the issues just mentioned bear some relation to the survey. With that as background, let me proceed to the survey itself. In so doing, I hope I can act as a voice for the many pastors who shared their ideas, insights, and feelings with us.

The survey posed six questions:

1. What are your most strongly felt convictions about the role of pastor?

2. What are your major concerns or anxieties about the role of pastor today?

3. What suggestions would you give bishops to support and develop pastors and their ministry?

4. What are your criteria for judging a pastor effective?

5. What are your suggestions for programs to prepare or update pastors today?

6. What are your suggestions regarding collaborative ministry, alternatives to traditional pastors, lay ministry, team ministry, and so on for the future?

A full report of the responses is printed in the January 1985 issue of *Church* magazine. Six main themes surfaced; they may be stated in the form of three tensions and three challenges for pastors.

1. *Pastors experience a growing tension between their dual roles as shepherds and spiritual leaders on the one hand and administrators of finances, buildings, and employees on the other.* One man wrote, "The pastor finds himself dissipated, nickeled and dimed to death. His authority and influence are diminished by bureaucratic committees. He is expected to raise the money and make ends meet and yet everyone else wants to tell him how to spend the money."

Another said, "I worry most about finances and administration because I'm neither trained for nor interested in these areas. However, this drain of energy causes me to cut corners on what I do best—people things, pastoral things. As a result I'm frustrated at both aspects of the job."

A third pastor said, "If you are expecting us to continue as at present, provide helpful courses in building construction, electrical engineering, boilers, personnel management, bookkeeping, record keeping, fund raising, purchasing, time management, etc., plus some refresher courses in theology, Scripture, group dynamics, psychology, and leadership skills."

2. *Pastors experience a growing tension from being the man in the middle between "the Church above" and "the Church below," between old and new expectations, between conservatives and liberals, and between individual staff members and/or lay volunteers who get involved in "turf fights."* One man said, "A pastor is often caught in the middle between the realities of the layperson's life and the rules and regulations of church authorities." Another said, "A pastor gets caught between old expectations and new ones. As a result he feels guilty and gets complaints from both sides. . . . It's hard to discern, set priorities, say 'no' without offending people."

And here is a string of brief observations from a variety of respondents: You are "subject to enormous expectations, many of which are mutually contradictory"; there is "increasing combat with unenlightened fundamentalism"; "Competition between priests, between staff members, between parishes, between parish organizations is petty, mean-spirited, debilitating." One man offered the hint of a solution, saying, "A good pastor is like a quarterback, a coach, an orchestra leader. He can't do it alone, but the others need a leader, a coordinator."

3. *Pastors experience a growing tension between keeping one eye on the long-range future and the other on the immediate needs of the present.* Many pastors see this as a creative tension, a stimulating opportunity. One said, "Being a pastor today puts a person in the enviable position of being the funnel of a tremendous number of new and exciting programs in the Church and the opportunity to put these into effect at the grass roots. The self-perception of pastors is that they are grossly undervalued when all the research points to the opposite conclusion." Another wrote, "Today's pastor needs to be a minister to a ministering community. He needs skills in (a) spotting, encouraging, developing talent in his people; (b) establishing effective structures for coordinating large numbers of people in diverse fields of activity; (c) providing ongoing stimulation, encouragement, and sense of purpose."

A third pastor made this comment: "We need to create situations where people will be able to try new things, make mistakes, and then get feedback rather than criticism in developing styles of ministry. As someone said, today's illegal activity often becomes tomorrow's great new breakthrough." Picking up the notion that creativity involves stretching the bounds of what is officially sanctioned, another pastor said, "We can't afford to train people for jobs only to have them told that they aren't allowed to do that for which they have been trained."

Thus, the three tensions: having the dual job of pastor and administrator; being the man in the middle; and living simultaneously in the present and the future. What are the three challenges today's pastor faces?

1. *The challenge of building an authentic community with a climate*

of effective communication. This challenge takes in such diverse subjects as effective Sunday bulletins; productive meetings and decision-making processes; two-way interaction between the local parish and the larger Church, communication with the secular society; and creative interaction between affluent and disadvantaged parishes.

One pastor said, "Our people need to be educated to accept the new style of pastoring required by Vatican II, the manpower shortage, new ministries, and so on." Another pursued that theme: "Preparation for celebrating 'priestless Sundays' will require good theology and sound practice. We need a well-thought-out process for preparing the general Catholic population for the radical shift that will inevitably take place when the number of priests dictates new parish models, new models of sacramental life, and who knows what else."

Regarding advice to bishops, one pastor had this to say: "Bishops should regularly and seriously meet with good, scholarly theologians of various schools to discern the times, then pass on to the pastors what they discover." Another suggested, "Facilitate the establishment of networks of pastors with whom they can relate, share, support, and dream about what the parish is and what it can become." A third pastor said, "Reverse the funnel relationship. Instead of us being at the bottom of your funnel, you should be at the bottom of ours. Find out what kinds of assistance and programs we need rather than using us as objects of your pet programs." On the worldwide level, one man said, "Bishops should not give up trying to get the pope to change some of the things I'd like to see changed in the Church. [We need] increased consultation with the troops in the trenches."

Creating a climate of open communication in a parish seems to be a key element in the job description that pastors put forth for themselves. Here are a few examples: a pastor should be "a good listener who can sort out what he hears and act upon that which is valuable, insightful." He should have "the courage to listen to his own homilies." A pastor needs "patience, a sense of humor, the ability to relate well to people, reasonable skills in organizing and getting people to work together, an ability to see the larger picture, reasonable ability to communicate and to preach." Another put it this way: "After almost 30 years, I still open and close doors, shut off lights, and lock and unlock the hall for people. Being available, attending two or three meetings some nights, being interrupted a lot—I guess those are signs of a good pastor." Finally, one pastor described a good parish as a place where "people are concerned about the parish next door and the parish across the ocean."

2. *The challenge of establishing spirituality or interiority as the root of the pastor's life as an individual and the parish's life as a community.* When speaking of spirituality, religious professionals can unconsciously slip into platitudes or generalities. The responses to the survey provide ample illustration. Nevertheless, a few quotations will give you a feeling for the tone of the pastors' comments. One said, "It's hard to find time and energy to do the real work of nourishing your own faith and spiri-

tuality in order to nourish that of the people. It's hard to give what you haven't got. And it's hard to get it if time is always drained by other things." Another remarked, a pastor has to "use Jesus and the Gospels as the main criteria for his ministry. I mean dependence on Jesus as the real pastor of our parish. . . ." A third said, a pastor ought to be "a man of faith who is in for the long haul, willing to take people where they are without complicating their already difficult lives; possessing the courage to confront when necessary and to make hard decisions and then take the flack; determined to grow personally, emotionally, spiritually; and respectful of himself without getting preoccupied with his own person."

Some priests articulated criteria for a good pastor in the form of questions: "Is he a man of hospitality, a man who is comfortable with himself and with others? Do people feel closer to God and to the Church because of him, or farther away? Do parishioners call to find out what Mass he has so they can attend it? Conversely, do they call so they can avoid it?" Another writer cautioned, however: "I fear abstract profiles of what I should be. I value a profile that recognizes the unique strengths and differences in each person, each parish, and as a result, each style of pastoring."

This same theme of diversity appears in the following remarks: "How does a priest or a pastor measure his success? Number of communions? Conversions? Perceived spiritual life of the congregation? The fact that the liturgy committee and the choir speak to one another? How can I prove to myself that I am a good priest and a competent pastor? The Church for which many older pastors were prepared doesn't exist anymore. How will they adapt? The Church we are training priests for today may not be the Church of tomorrow. How can we help them (and ourselves) be visionaries who can encourage and accept change?"

3. *The challenge of collaborative ministry with nonordained persons, especially women.* Attitudes on this matter varied from enthusiasm to caution to defensiveness. Take these statements, for example: "My parish staff has ten people right now, and I see it branching out even more. Five are women. It's the only way to go. The future is here already"; "Working with women (lay or religious) is something that many priests find threatening. How do we deal with it in a creative way?"

Some other observations. One pastor wrote, "Many parishes are already immersed in collaborative ministry. Experimentation in a variety of forms is not just a nice alternative; it's an absolute necessity. Pastoral ministry without a true 'pastor' is nonsense, but there's no reason to restrict the role of pastor to male celibates." Another raised a question: "I see women playing a more and more prominent role in the religious life of congregations. What then will happen to the men who traditionally back off when women begin to play a more prominent role? We could go from a male-dominated Church to a female-dominated Church. And the Church would not be well served by that eventuality."

As usual, some pastors asked very practical questions: "How will this new ministry be financed? I think total reliance on volunteer help can be a dead end. Good people, professionally trained and competently employed—and justly remunerated—will be the secret of success in large parishes in the years to come." Finally, one respondent raised an issue that is appearing more frequently: "To respond to the shortage, I would favor a look at the question of a married clergy. It seems we are willing to sacrifice sacramental life for celibacy."

These three challenges—community, interiority, and collaboration—coupled with the three tensions, represent the main themes of the survey of Chicago pastors. To augment them, let me summarize the results of the two subsequent meetings conducted by the pastors themselves.

At the first gathering in June 1984, the 50 participants pooled their experiences to draw a thumbnail sketch of parish life in these changing times. They drew up six conclusions.

1. *Parishioners are increasingly independent in forming their spiritual and moral values. They don't automatically accept positions set forth in official church teaching.* This conclusion is corroborated by Dr. Leege's analysis: "American individualism is a pervasive value that affects not only how people approach God, but how they deal with one another." He cites as an example the routine dismissal of Catholic social teachings by American Catholics. An even more obvious example is the repudiation of papal teaching on birth control.

2. *In the same way, the pastor does not have automatic moral authority locally. While still the pivotal person in parish life, he must earn his leadership position by the quality of his spirituality, his homilies, his decisions, his ideas.* Again, this seems consistent with Dr. Leege's finding that "when asked to rank the trait parishioners most value in a pastor, they ranked sensitivity to the needs of others by a wide margin" over the alternatives. "They want a pastor who understands them, who consults them, who respects them as contributors to the common life of the parish."

3. *As the priest shortage begins to strike the parish, the leadership vacuum is filled by a plethora of unordained ministers. The pastor is challenged to coordinate these ministers' work, resolve conflicts, and provide training and ongoing development.* The Notre Dame study supports this observation: "Probably few of us are fully aware of the extent to which we depend on women to conduct the ministries, programs, and activities of Catholic parishes in the United States. Fifty-eight percent of the respondents identified a woman as the most influential leader in the parish aside from the pastor."

4. *Parishes tend to be increasingly more polarized, both vertically and horizontally.* Someone has said that we are Roman Catholic Christians. Depending on which of those three words individual parishioners emphasize, they will have very different ecclesiological positions. Keeping all three in proper balance is a challenge for any pastor.

The Chicago pastors discussed polarization in statements like these: "Don't leave us to die in the desert of nonsupport and hostility which results when the far right attacks"; and "I continually have to apologize for the sinfulness, especially that of sexism, that exists within the Church itself." In a parish of 2,000 families a pastor may be assaulted by a handful of people or even one individual who pounds away at him day after day about an issue that isn't of prime importance to the bulk of his parishioners.

5. *Spiritual nourishment depends less on "ex opere operato" sacraments than on the perceived quality of Sunday liturgies and homilies. Moreover, specialized experiences such as Cursillo, Christ Renews His Parish, RENEW, and Marriage Encounter play an increasingly important part in the spirituality of our people.* This conclusion is consistent with Dr. Searle's discussion of the boundaries between Catholics in good standing and those who are not, the manner of making moral decisions, and the decline in the use of the sacrament of reconciliation. He says, "Paradoxically, the reason why the practice of sacramental penance is in decline may well be in part that preachers and teachers have put such emphasis on interiority and so little emphasis on ecclesial identity and vocation. By playing down the role of penance as reconciliation with the Church, . . . we may in fact be collaborating with the individualism of our culture to undermine the public, social, and sacramental character of the Catholic tradition."

I agree, but would make a further comment. Some of the responses to the Chicago pastors' survey indicate a serious deterioration in the relationship between what many have called "the Church above" and "the Church below." Speaking of bishops, some wrote, "Try not to treat pastors as lower-level employees at the chancery office." Another said, "I'm not trying to be a wise guy, but I mean it when I say just don't complicate things or get in the way." We heard: "I feel that church discipline is given more emphasis than the Gospel"; and "There are too many taboo subjects in the Church." One pastor said that the pope and bishops need "increased consultation with the troops in the trenches." What comes across is a strong sense that pastors would like some credible way of sharing their experience of what is authentically spiritual nourishment for themselves and for their people. They do not perceive themselves as listened to or taken seriously. I mention this as another possible element, besides the individualism of our culture, that contributes to an emphasis on interiority to the neglect of ecclesial identity. Both factors should be carefully examined and addressed.

6. *Young people are becoming less involved in and committed to the Church.* Again this seems to dovetail with one of the most consistent responses of parishioners as reflected in the Notre Dame study. They want to be sure that the parish has as one of its top priorities the discovery of more effective ways of handing on the faith to the next generation. Grandparents grieve about grandchildren who go unbaptized because their parents no longer attend Mass. Parents grieve about high school or college students who have dropped out of the Church.

Thus the results of our research. Where do we go from here? I'd like to make five specific recommendations, which flow from this material.

1. We need to set up pilot programs for recruiting and training men and women for the new role of parish business manager. A special constellation of practical business skills, coupled with theological and ministerial skills, must be developed if this new staff person is to be completely effective.

2. We need to develop grant programs to assist poor parishes, especially in inner-city areas, that desperately need business managers and other staff. Unfortunately, such parishes often have the oldest, least efficient physical plants, the greatest human needs, and the fewest resources.

3. We need to develop effective training programs for new pastors and for veteran pastors who need to learn new skills. Moreover, we must recognize that the pastors of the future will more and more include permanent deacons, women, laypeople, and married couples.

4. We need to develop creative programs to address the special challenges and opportunities that face men and women working collaboratively in ministry.

5. We need to develop effective ways of educating our Catholic people about the changes in the modern Church. How can we help them prepare for the future? How can we assist them to read the signs of the times not as disasters for the Church but as the work of the Holy Spirit leading us into new ways of being the people of God?

I'd like to conclude by sharing with you some words from the second of the two meetings that the pastors conducted after our survey was completed. One pastor said, "At Sunday Mass we have all kinds of people: rich, poor, educated, uneducated, sinful people, pious people all coming together. They don't surrender themselves to humanism or social science. They surrender themselves to the presence of God, the reality of Jesus in the liturgy. It is there on Sunday in the Eucharist that I find my own faith in Jesus grounded and expressed. It is then lived out by all of us in our various milieux during the coming week."

Another pastor shared this experience: "When I came as the new pastor, the parishioners said, 'Father, we have survived all kinds of pastoral styles: chaotic, rigid, uncertain, healthy. We like our parish. You are welcome to join us.' I did so and it has worked out well. It is in that tenacity and resilience of believing people that I find the spirit of Jesus at work." For me this is a good description of what a parish is and who a pastor is: tenacious, resilient, faith filled, an instrument through which the spirit of Jesus works.

Editor's Note: Fr. Ventura's talk was a luncheon address and no transcription was made of the session. This chapter is based on Fr. Ventura's written text.

PARISH LEADERSHIP

SPEAKER

Fr. Philip J. Murnion
Director, National Pastoral Life Center

PANEL

Fr. George E. Crespin
Chancellor, Diocese of Oakland

Fr. Leo T. Mahon
Pastor, St. Victor's Parish
Calumet City, Illinois

Mr. Eugene Tozzi
Parish Team Minister, Sts. John and Paul Parish
Larchmont, New York

Sr. Barbara Garland, SC
Vicar for Religious and Priests, Diocese of Syracuse

Mr. A. Robert Garofalo
Member, Our Lady of Mercy Parish
Park Ridge, New Jersey

It could be argued that the central issue for the Church today is leadership: the numbers and composition of those in leadership, the shift in leadership style proposed by Vatican II, and the dynamics of leadership in church life. Sharp decline in the numbers of priests and religious will not soon change. There has been a sharp increase, at the same time, in the number of permanent deacons and full-time lay ministers in the Church. And there remains considerable tension regarding the roles for women in parish and church life. These changes in number and composition of leadership mean that parishes increasingly have fewer or no full-time priests, that responsibility for ministerial leadership is shifting to religious and laity, and that preparation for ministry has new requirements.

There have also been serious changes in styles of leadership since Vatican II. The Council proposed that hierarchy and leadership be reinterpreted within the context of the Church as the people of God. Second, leadership is to be exercised in a style that is, depending on circumstances, collegial, consultative, and enabling of the general leadership of all the baptized. This means that the role of the laity, within the church community and in regard to the mission of the Church in the world, is to be respected and encouraged.

Besides numbers and style, the dynamics of leadership deserve careful attention. The NCCB Parish Project confirmed the view that nothing affects a parish more than its pastor. Even when the ministerial leadership of laity and religious is expanded, the pastor's leadership responsibility increases.

More complicated questions about the nature of church leadership could also be discussed. I want to advert to some of these issues, though we can say little about them given the data currently available. Some would argue for a more prophetic kind of leadership, challenging the American Catholic people. Some would argue for a more priestly function, assembling, gathering, nurturing. Some see leadership as essentially a teaching role, while some expect the leader to animate and organize the gifts and energies that exist in the Church. Some look for a very protective ministry, others for a ministry that takes Christianity and the Church into very risky waters. Choices about the nature and function of church leadership are being made with very little or no public discussion, much less consensus. While the data of the study will reveal some of the preferences of current leaders and parishioners, they do not enable us to come to completely satisfactory conclusions about church leadership. While it is important to be clear about our achievements in this study, it is also important that we recognize its limitations.

Given that preamble, let me move into the discussion. I will examine the composition of today's parish staff, the volunteer leaders, the dynamics between staff and volunteers, and the spread and effectiveness of councils and decision making in parishes. What can we say about the leadership in terms of carrying out the work of the parish and in terms of decisions about the parish? Who are these pastors, associate pastors, women religious and laity in staff positions, and parish volunteers? How are they prepared for their roles? How do they work through the issues that arise from their status and place in the Church?

As I said, modern parishes generally feature a decreasing number of priests and a growing number of deacons, religious and laity in full-time and part-time staff positions. Moreover, a small but growing number of parishes have no full-time priest at all. But people do not live in parishes in general; they are members of particular parishes. There are considerable differences among these parishes.

Three percent of the parishes in the United States have no full-time priest; more than half have one full-time priest; 25% have two full-time priests; and about 20% have three or more full-time priests. In many parts of the country, the major distinction is between parishes staffed by religious orders and those staffed by the diocese. The order is more likely to ensure that there is at least a minimal community of two priests in the rectory.

About 25% of the parishes have permanent deacons, though these are rarely full-time parish ministers. One-third have sisters in parish ministry, not counting the sisters serving in schools. And about 30% have laypersons serving in professional pastoral positions.

Not surprisingly, it is the larger parishes that tend to have the larger staffs. More particularly, the suburban parishes have not only numbers but money with which to hire staffs. As noted in Parish Project reports, we should be aware of staffing inequalities among parishes, now that staffs are likely to be hired rather than appointed. It also seems true that, while religious and deacons and in some very few instances laypeople are used as a parish director where there is no full-time priest, the increase in this practice is a function not so much of priest shortage as of changing theology and expanding ministry. It is the parish with more than one priest that is likely to employ religious and lay staff. Religious and lay staff members also appear more frequently outside the Northeast, in the Midwest, Southwest and South Central states. Northeastern parishes have a stronger clerical tradition, which seems to militate against expansion of the roles of laity and religious. Furthermore, there are many externe clergy, clergy from other countries or other parts of this country serving in northeastern parishes. They are effectively freelance clergy who make private arrangements with pastors.

The schools remain the primary apostolate for sisters. Forty percent of parishes have sisters in their schools. And where sisters are in other parish ministries, that ministry is usually religious education. While many sisters have left schools to go into other work, the extent of the shift is exaggerated. Most have remained committed to education at a time when the ratio of children in parochial schools to those in religious education programs has changed in favor of the latter. Moreover, many if not most of the sisters in other positions were placed there by priests and bishops.

It is evident from the work of the Parish Project and its successor, the National Pastoral Life Center, that a significant and growing portion of parish staff leadership is not directly recruited and monitored by the bishops or diocesan offices. While in some few dioceses personnel offices assume responsibility for all pastoral personnel—clergy, laity, and religious—in most the recruitment, screening, hiring, and working conditions of nonordained parish personnel and of externe clergy are the responsibility of individual pastors and parishes. Given the growing number of such parish ministers and their impact on the ministry of the Church, and given the demands of justice both for the parish and for those who serve it, bishops and diocesan offices should take more responsibility for the recruitment and preparation of parish ministers. At present there are few, if any, standards regarding preparation or even regarding ministry itself. We will return to this matter later.

A few other matters of concern regarding staffs. The question of the proper role of permanent deacons remains. This must be settled through experience. The evolution of the role of the deacon will have some impact on parish staffing and leadership.

Second, there is a tendency in some parts of the country to invite religious orders to take responsibility for more parishes. This trend needs to be monitored. For while religious orders have in the past, do now, and will in the future make an important contribution to parish life—in some areas they are its mainstay—parish work is neither the particular apostolate nor the priority of many orders. This creates a temptation to staff parishes with men who simply do not fit the order's own primary ministry.

Third, a growing number of laity wish to make a commitment to a life of church ministry in general rather than to some specialty like religious education or social work. Unfortunately, the Church does not have the capacity at present to receive such a commitment and to make the necessary reciprocal commitment. There is an exception to this. One can construe the permanent diaconate as a mechanism for laymen to make and receive such a commitment. However, this option is not available to women or to men who may wish to marry later on. The Church will be pressed in the future to provide for such ministry commitments. An especially important group in this regard, I think, are the wives of permanent deacons. Many may have been more active than their husbands in the past and may have gone through all or most of the training their husbands received.

Finally, absentee pastors who provide the sacraments must not be considered a permanently acceptable solution to the shortage of priests. Priests are no more likely to find this satisfying than parishioners are. Moreover, such a change could appreciably alter the sacramental style of Catholic pastoral life.

The leadership of parishes is adequately described only when we include parishioners who accept positions of responsibility for various parish works. As a matter of fact, even this will not tell the whole story, for the parish acts in many ways that are never recognized as formal ministries. The full story of leadership would have to include the very many ways people enable others to live more fully through their acts of charity and justice, through their enterprise and community involvement. At least one parish I know has acknowledged this fact through an annual night of appreciation for all those who serve the community.

If we count all who fill positions of responsibility in parishes, beyond pastors, we find that 83% of the leaders are lay and, of course, most of them are volunteers. That so many laypeople are involved in parish life and ministry is not new; what is new are the types of ministries in which they are involved and the weight of responsibility they carry. As we know, laypeople have new responsibilities in liturgy and other ministries. Further, laypeople exercise greater responsibility than once was the case. In some matters they appear to have the last word, and in many matters the pastor will consult with them before taking any action. Finally, laypeople are part of the basic leadership team in some parishes, even though they are not paid staff.

Volunteers tend to be very active people. Twenty-five percent of them take part in four or more parish activities, and 60% participate in two to four activities. Less than 20% restrict their involvement to one activity. They put in a good bit of time, some almost as much as the pastor. More than 50% give at least 15 hours a month to the parish. It is not that they have nothing else to do; they are otherwise very busy, since the majority are married, employed, and tend to have large families. It is the old story: recruit the busy person.

The volunteers are usually long-time parishioners, somewhat better educated than the average parishioner, and somewhat more centrist; fewer liberals and conservatives volunteer their time and talents. Volunteers are also slightly more likely to be converts.

Not surprisingly, volunteers feel more attached to the parish than the average parishioner, and they have not adopted the storied cynicism of the insider or rectory habitué. They are much more appreciative of the liturgy and preaching and indeed of the spiritual and social life of the parish than are most parishioners. Furthermore, volunteer leaders are only half as likely to find fault with the most disputed liturgical reforms: the sign of peace, communion in the hand and from the cup, lay lectors, and eucharistic ministers. The volunteers consider the parish their community and are twice as likely as others to find their friends among fellow parishioners. They are most often recruited by the pastor or some other member of the staff and are happy to be involved.

Much has been made of the preponderance of women among active parishioners and parish leadership, both as staff and volunteers. This element has been singled out in reports and became headlines in some diocesan newspaper accounts of the Notre Dame study. It is true that the leaders tend to be women. More remarkable, however, is that the Catholic Church generally attracts a higher ratio of men than do other Christian Churches, and that men are almost as likely as women to take leadership positions as long as they are already parish members. There is, of course, a danger of feminization of the Church—as there is in most religions—but we should be encouraged that we can reach so many men and that, if they stay attached to the parish, they may well take some leadership position. They will take different leadership positions than the women do, but they will take leadership positions. I am concerned about a self-fulfilling prophecy with respect to the feminization question. We could talk ourselves into believing that men will not get involved and then not seek to get men involved. Since most of the volunteer leaders are recruited, it will be important to recruit men and to recruit them to a variety of parish activities.

What do the volunteer leaders do? In order of frequency, they work on social programs, sit on parish councils, teach in religious education programs, and serve as eucharistic ministers. Volunteers are devoted and loyal parishioners, generous with their time and money; their families contribute significantly more to the parish than the average family. They are appreciative of the pastor, the staff, and the spiritual and social life of the parish. They do what needs to be done, and in many ministries in most parishes they are the people to whom their fellow parishioners look for leadership.

It is basic Catholic education and participation in church life that most prepare parishioners for ministry. They know the parish; they have been involved for a time and come to parish work with family and work experience, as well as more education than the average parishioner. They have had on the average five hours of specific preparation for what they do in the parish; one in five preparation hours occurs in workshops and one in twenty in catechist or other lay ministry training programs. The volunteers do not evince any great desire for more preparation.

Parish volunteers seem to get along with their pastors and with the staff, feeling that they can exercise influence on decisions and that the pastor tends to share decision making. Of course, were they seriously discontented, they might quit; "contented volunteers" may be a redundancy.

How well do parish leadership, pastor, staff, and volunteers meet the needs of the parishioners? Eighty percent of core parishioners feel that their spiritual needs are met completely or very well. Almost two-thirds find that the parish meets their social needs equally well; the rest, for the most part, are not looking to the parish for social activity. If we posit that fulfilling specifically spiritual goals is the main purpose of the parish and that community building is important, the parish is successful. Not only are parishioners' spiritual needs met, but the vast majority find at least some sense of community in their parishes; for more than half, this sense of community is strong. Again, there may be some redundancy in these findings. Catholics have clearly acquired a much more voluntary disposition toward church teaching and church participation; and the acutely dissatisfied may simply have walked away because their own lives or parish performance discouraged further participation.

It remains true, nevertheless, that core parishioners are predominantly satisfied with parish life. Fifty percent are reasonably content with the homilies, though only 25% seem genuinely impressed or moved by them. Two-thirds are satisfied with the liturgy. They will generally turn to the parish staff for help in times of grief or doubt, though not as readily when problems require professional help or assistance in finding a job.

Elements in parish life warranting more attention include religious education of the young, outreach to the unchurched and alienated, help for those dependent on alcohol or drugs, and help for the poor of the parish. I am not in a position to report parishioners' opinions on various church teachings, but this data will become available in the future.

As far as the parish priest is concerned, parishioners want a sensitive and holy man who does not hide his humanity. They most want him to display these qualities in celebrating the liturgy and in preaching, which remain the key priestly functions in the minds of parishioners.

In general, the view of parish leadership held by registered parishioners is a fairly positive one. Oh, the preaching could be improved (it is important, perhaps more important than ever), and continual effort must be made to respect people's views and needs. But parish leadership is not doing badly at all, especially when we consider how skeptical people have become about institutions in general.

A word about the decision-making process. Parish councils have been established in perhaps three-fourths of the parishes, but they have yet to become all they were expected to be. When the staffs of the 1,100 parishes in the study were asked to identify the five factors with the greatest impact on the parish, less than 5% placed council on the list. This finding is not as surprising as it appears at first glance. Other institutions which similarly established constituent councils in the late 1960s are not doing any better. Universities with their faculty senates, hospitals with their community boards, or corporate boards of directors with their public-interest members have hardly set a glowing example of participatory decision making.

Though parish councils have a long way to go and may be in a second generation of development, parishioners do report that the pastor consults with various people before making most decisions. He may consult the council or a specific committee or board, or he may consult other members of the staff and leadership, but he is far less likely to act entirely on his own.

Some of our Parish Project work on the most effective parishes in the country showed that the extent to which pastors engage parishioners in decision making and ministry has an effect on the entire parish. While there is a long way to go before parishioner responsibility for policy and practice becomes a reality, the journey is worth it. Not only is this arrangement more faithful both to the theology of Vatican II and the dictates of the times, it is also likely to produce satisfied and active parishioners (and more solvent parishes).

Obviously, leadership is a matter of relationships. The parish features relationships between pastor and parishioners, between pastor and staff members, between other leaders and the parishioners, and so forth. Volunteers seem to feel that difficulties that arise within the staff generally get worked out, and they describe the relationship among all those in leadership as fairly good.

Yet, the further development of parish life and leadership calls for new styles and skills on the part of all concerned. Those who exercise leadership in parish life, especially the pastor, will have to be both convinced and competent when it comes to fostering shared responsibility among all those who minister to the parish. Besides being a leader of leaders, the pastor will have his specific role to play as the religious leader of the parish. Those who exercise leadership will also need specific competence in the area of their responsibility as well as attitudes and skills that favor a collaborative style. The new programs for pastors that are slowly developing around the country need to be expanded and perhaps made more consistently mandatory for priests who are going to be pastors. As the Code of Canon Law indicates, parish ministers have a similar right and obligation to obtain the preparation they need for their ministry. In these various ways, parish leadership has to be prepared for their new relationships and styles of relationships, and for the work they must do and the way they must do it.

As I have said, the expansion of the leadership roles of laity and religious does not diminish the leadership of the priest but increases it and gives it new scope. Where priests have been replaced by religious and laity as full-time parish directors, parishioners have reacted by saying that, while they appreciate the leadership of the new director, they still want a resident priest. There is no danger that expansion of the leadership of others will eliminate the need for priests. It does place new burdens on priests, however. It also puts pressure on those who exercise leadership at other levels of the Church to adopt new styles of leadership, both to set an example and to preserve consistency.

Much more will be forthcoming about leadership from the Notre Dame study. But much is already evident, and the promise is great. We have come a long way in parish studies. A generation ago, Fr. Joseph Fichter offered the Church great insight from his in-depth study of one parish, *Southern Parish*, and his later analysis, *Social Relations in the Urban Parish*. Joseph Schuyler somewhat imitated his model in *Northern Parish*, a study of a parish in the Bronx. In the decades that followed, Andrew Greeley and others offered the Church considerable data on the thought and behavior of American Catholics. He and his associates further examined the nature of parish life in a book dealing with three Chicago parishes. Thomas Sweetser, besides his dissertation on Chicago parishes, has published reports based on the parishes where his organization has provided consulting services. Now, after surveying a sample of all the parishes of the country, we will have an opportunity to examine a combination of parishioners' views and parish dynamics through an in-depth analysis of 36 carefully chosen parishes that mirror the diversity of the American Catholic landscape.

PANEL DISCUSSION

DR. BUTLER: Our moderator this afternoon is Fr. George Crespin, chancellor of the Diocese of Oakland. Fr. Crespin is well qualified to lead us. Not only is he chairman of the National Association of Church Personnel Administrators, but he has also served for nearly 20 years in pastoral assignments in the diocese. He is a native of New Mexico and was ordained in 1962. Fr. Crespin is a graduate of St. Patrick Seminary in Menlo Park, California and has done advanced studies at Notre Dame.

FR. CRESPIN: As Dr. Butler says, I am from New Mexico, whose history reaches back before the Declaration of Independence. Now I am in California, which has the highest Hispanic population in the United States. I look forward to that proposed study on the Hispanic Catholic Church. It will provide some very important insights for the future of the Church at large.

Let me say a few words about Fr. Murnion before getting to the panel. When the dust settles, perhaps in the next century, and the history of the Church in America, especially the history of the American parish, is written, Fr. Murnion's name is going to appear again and again. He has been most instrumental in getting us to reflect on the nature of the parish, on its past and future. His talk has helped all of us understand more clearly what elements make up a good parish in the United States today.

The first respondent to Fr. Murnion's presentation will be Fr. Leo Mahon. I had the privilege of meeting Fr. Mahon for the first time this morning, although I have been hearing about him for 25 years. Even when I was in seminary, his name was well known on the West Coast, particularly after he moved to Panama and began his ministry there. A great deal of excitement followed the San Miguelito experiment, because it held out a lot of hope to the rest of us. Fr. Mahon has proved in the last 25 years to be an effective leader. Even more important, perhaps, he has brought out leadership qualities in people of two different cultures, that of Panama and that of the American Midwest. He is presently pastor of St. Victor's Parish in Calumet City, Illinois.

FR. MAHON: The theme of this conference delights me, because I feel the parish may be the only true entity in the Catholic Church. The parish is where the people gather, where they are affected, where they come together to worship, to heal and forgive one another, to pass on their dream. I think we ought to be far more careful talking about deaneries, and vicariates, dioceses, and even the Vatican as real entities in the lives of people. People have some curiosity about these structures, but they do not find them very meaningful.

I remember a few years ago being asked by a bishops' committee for help on a certain project. It turned out that, as usual, they wanted to write a document. I asked if they knew that almost no one reads these documents. They said yes, but decided to go ahead anyway. My point is that getting information to the people is a real problem. Even diocesan newspapers and agencies have little influence on the people in a parish. Most people in this country read their parish bulletin—whether it is good or bad—but most don't ever see a diocesan newspaper or a religious magazine.

I would also take slight issue with the phrase "core Catholic." I understand what Fr. Murnion means by it, but I would suggest that we have overly associated piety with the concept of *practicing* Catholic. Those who are devout, those who go to Mass on Sunday, are considered practicing Catholics. We organize parishes on that assumption. In so doing we say to people that piety is the only door into the Christian community, the Catholic Christian community. I think there are others.

In our own parish, and in other places I have been, when an unemployment commission or some truly effective program of care for the poor starts in the parish, people who never come to Mass show up. They say, "If this is what you are doing, count us in." These other doors don't appear very much in this survey.

I live in Calumet City, in a large steel-producing area, the largest on the continent. Unemployment is high. I remember when parishioners surveyed unemployed people, asking if they would like some help. Thirty men attended the first meeting at the rectory. I knew only two of them, but they all knew me. They were parishioners, but inactive ones. Many of them now come to Mass because they felt somebody cared. The same applies to those involved in substance abuse and other problems. I think we ought to consider some new paths for the future.

There is danger of a reaction. At one of our periodic open meetings, a lady who doesn't like my style of leadership got up and said, "You know, there were never any drunks or poor in this parish until you came."

It is not the Eucharist that bridges the pious Catholic, the sacramental Catholic, and the socially aware Catholic. It is reconciliation. In Panama and Latin America, I had something to do with the emergence of the Basic Christian Communities and in my view the single most significant development in the Catholic Church is the new opening to reconciliation. I don't think we should keep it under a bushel any longer. People need to come together, to feel a sense of sin, a sense of forgiveness and reconciliation. At Easter and Christmas in our parish, we had 400 private confessions and 2,600 people at the communal penance services. Twenty-six hundred adults: young people, people who hadn't been in church in years, men who hadn't been to confession in 23 years. I think that is extraordinary. To my mind, reconciliation is the paradigm of the sacraments, not baptism, not even Eucharist.

I think priestly leadership has to become corporate. Most priests do not know how to run a new parish. They have never even seen one successfully launched. I would recommend sending in a team, a priest plus two or three people with the right skills, to get the parish started. I think in this archdiocese we spend two or three million dollars a year on a seminary system that produces 15 priests. I am not objecting to that, but we need thousands and thousands of lay ministers trained in the Bible and in relationships, especially in the Hispanic community. Why don't we do it?

Let me close by saying that I slightly disagree with the survey's findings. The drive for participation, equality, and ordination on the part of women in my perception is far stronger than the survey indicates. I think it is building into a mighty wind, either a cyclone that may destroy the Church or the mighty wind that reforms it.

FR. CRESPIN: Our next panelist is Gene Tozzi. He is the coordinator of religious education at SS. John and Paul Church in Larchmont, New York. He served for 11 years in that capacity under a variety of pastors and staffing arrangements. He is presently exploring the issue of leadership and staff organization in the parish as a doctoral student in the church leadership program at Fordham University's Graduate School of Education.

MR. TOZZI: There are three issues I would like to address. One is the issue of leadership and staffing in the parish. A second is the question of the needs of families in parishes. How do you allow for these needs in staffing parishes, especially when pastors have a list of 18 ministries that they have been told a full-time person should be handling? Third is the question of lay commitment to ministry, which Fr. Murnion raised very perceptively in his paper.

My studies lately at Fordham have been in the area of leadership and staff leadership. It is interesting to note that, while the students are mostly people in education and church work, we are reading business and management. I began with a negative view of the word *management,* but I am emerging with a very positive concept. Management is basically helping people to do effectively what they are there to do and helping them find the resources to succeed. The notion of good management, properly understood, needs to penetrate the Church a bit more. I am pleased to hear there is the beginning of some training for pastors in management and leadership skills. I fear that in many places the training you get as an associate pastor does not prepare you well for being a pastor. The monarchical pastor of many years ago is a thing of the past in some places. The poor man is so glad to have an associate these days that he is not going to ask too much. Perhaps, he is even afraid to offer guidance because things are so different.

Pastors and all parish staff members need training in the area of collaboration and working together. I read some material on working with blue-collar workers that suggested why the Japanese make better cars than we do—if that is indeed the case. People call together blue-collar workers on the factory floor and hold a staff meeting once a week. Everybody has the right to put things on the agenda. Is somebody driving the forklift too fast? Are you piling your cartons too high? Are you running the assembly line the wrong way? Everyone has the opportunity to put things on the agenda and get those issues out and have them discussed. American management is beginning to learn that this open style is a better way to make cars or widgets or whatever.

Church workers see themselves as being concerned about relationships. Yet how many parishes have no staff meeting? How often is everything handled on a one-on-one basis between the pastor and each staff member? For a period of time I had a pastor who held staff meetings; these months were among my most productive. Unfortunately, the man is now dead. I am changing jobs because I found I am more productive when the staff meets and shares ideas. The pastor does not even have to preside all the time. Each staff member, in turn, can take the opportunity to chair the meeting and present the agenda. The pastor can sit back and think, rather than always being on the spot. We need to work on skills like these.

The needs of family and ministry to family deserve attention. My wife has been a family minister for two years in a parish and unfortunately the position is the first one to be cut when budget problems arise. How do we approach those needs with the limited resources we have? How can laypeople make a commitment to lifetime ministry in the Church and be affirmed in that commitment through the bishop? How can the Church, in turn, be committed to us? A lot of people want to give and receive such a commitment, but the vehicle is not yet there.

FR. CRESPIN: Our next panelist is Sr. Barbara Garland, a member of the Sisters of Charity. I have had the pleasure of knowing Sr. Garland for several years through our participation in the National Association of Church Personnel Administrators. She was at one time president of that organization. Presently, she is vicar for personnel in the Diocese of Syracuse in New York, and in that capacity she is department chairman for the director for priest personnel, the vicar for religious, the co-director for vocation and seminarian programs, and the director for ministerial formation. So she has a grasp of all the problems involved in personnel work, as well as some of the solutions.

SR. GARLAND: The study data reveal what many of us are now experiencing: a massive shift in personnel in the Church. There is great change in role definitions, in functions, in job descriptions; the study certainly reflects this change on the parish level.

We have a new expression in the Church: "priestless parish." The study has added something to my perspective, so that I would like to change that expression to "priest-filled parish." One of the questions I would raise—I don't know if the data can resolve it—is whether parishes have lay ministers by design or by default. Do I hire a layperson because I do not have an associate or a sister or a brother available, or do I choose a layperson because of the lay vocation in the Church? That is a serious question for the parish.

Given my work with church personnel administrators, I am interested in a comprehensive approach to understanding church personnel. No longer can dioceses have vocational offices that concentrate on priests and religious. The vocation of the laity and that of the permanent deacon have to be part of that comprehensive approach. Compensation and benefit programs, particularly transferable pensions for laypeople, require a lot of study and a lot of funding help. Training and formation programs must also take a comprehensive approach so that a seminarian experiences the perspective of a religious sister, a brother, or a layperson. The whole interactive system should lead to an understanding of collaboration, an understanding of men and women working together in ministry.

With new personnel, a major issue is allowing the person who has the job to make the decision. I did a study in our own diocese, exploring with some lay ministers what issues they thought important with regard to their staff positions. I thought compensation would be mentioned most often. Surprisingly, the principal issue was being excluded from major decisions that affected their service on the staff. The decisions were handled in the rectory or the convent and the lay minister was simply not consulted. The dimension of comprehensive, collaborative decision making at the parish level takes on new importance when you increase the involvement of laypersons as paid staff or even as volunteers.

I would raise a few other questions about the study. How is leadership defined? I think I see two definitions at work. On the one hand, the leader is someone who performs a public activity, like a eucharistic minister or a lector. On the other, the leader is one involved in decision making. I think the data should be examined in terms of those two roles.

I fear that this study could make a certain definition of the parish normative. I would like the Church to adopt a broad vision of the parish for the future. I don't know if the parish is always going to be where there is a church where a liturgy is celebrated. I don't see this study moving into creative forms of parish life. I don't know if it can do so.

One expansion of the study I would like to see is a real look at parish staff: what their issues are, how they are viewed by the volunteers, and how they are incorporated into the life of the parish. What are the implications of the graying of the Church? The average core leadership person is 49 years old. There are very little data on youth, who are the future of the Church. What does this mean? Finally, I cannot conclude without referring to Fr. Murnion's remarks on the feminization of the Church. Would that this feminization would penetrate every level of the Church.

FR. CRESPIN: Our final panelist is Gary Garofalo, who comes to us from the business world. Mr. Garofalo has 25 years of experience in creating and directing a full range of corporate public affairs programs and activities aimed at the achievement of strategic objectives. He has also been heavily involved in church structures, particularly parish councils and archdiocesan pastoral councils, and presently serves on the council in his home archdiocese. At the same time, Mr. Garofalo is chairman of the National Advisory Council to the bishops of the United States.

MR. GAROFALO: I will restrict my comments to lay leadership, leaving aside pastors and staff teams. I realize that strong lay leadership inevitably affects what pastors and their teams do, but I cannot deal in the time allotted with all these ramifications.

I am uncomfortable with the study in some ways. For one thing, the report seems to make ministry and leadership synonymous, and I am not sure this is valid. Obviously many ministries involve leadership, but I don't know that an usher or a song leader or a eucharistic minister is a parish leader in the true sense of the word. I agree with Sr. Garland that parish leadership needs to be defined.

Dr. Leege noted earlier that doing is leading. I would be quite concerned if we accepted that statement without qualification. In a sense, doing is leading, but if the people who are doing are not doing the right thing, I would not want to follow. I am very anxious to hear more about the style of leadership in future reports on the survey data.

As Dr. Dolan said, the laity have long been involved in parish activities. However, there has been much new activity since Vatican II. As a result, leadership is splintered. In my view, there has been no serious attempt to build a community among the leaders, the core group, if you will. If there is a leadership community, should it not be the parish council? Why hasn't the parish council affected the parish? It seems to me that many people come to the council, as they do in many ministries, with their own vested interest, their own little piece of the pie. Nothing is done to educate them in their role as baptized Catholics. I think the Church has to provide for this need.

Some steps are being taken that echo the old Christian Family Movement days when you made a continuing long-term commitment to some kind of formation before assuming a role in the parish. The RENEW program is providing such formation; it should be continued and expanded.

I am concerned about the gospel values that the Church is supposed to be promoting. What has happened to the pastoral statement on war and peace in terms of our parishes? Or the pastorals on racism and Hispanics? I don't see leadership attempting to bring these messages alive. The Notre Dame study shows that only 20% of parishes have social action programs and only 27% provide leadership training. The parish has to think about building a leadership community. I would make this a top priority.

FR. CRESPIN: I would now like to open the floor for questions and comments to Fr. Murnion or any member of the panel, after which Fr. Murnion will make some concluding remarks.

PARTICIPANT: I am Fr. Ray Kemp from Washington. I haven't heard a word in these presentations as to how parishes help people understand or interpret what they do at work. There is discussion of family, of evangelization, of passing on the faith. But, are we missing the importance of the world of work? Isn't that where folks spend a lot of their time? Fr. Mahon talked about unemployment. What about employment? Does the parish address what people do in the workplace in any way? Does it deal with the ethical questions, the moral questions, the questions of living?

FR. MAHON: In our parish, we try to do something on the ethical issues surrounding sex and work, especially with young people. On the other hand, I think that one of the reasons people are active in church, in a steelworker parish like ours, is to forget about work, to get away, to be important. I agree, though, that we haven't addressed these issues enough.

MR. GAROFALO: It seems to me that if individual formation programs and leadership training programs touched all the gospel values, you would bring those into the workplace with you.

FR. MURNION: I agree that the problem exists. I have been hunting for effective parish programs of this sort for a long time. Fr. Joyce has done some work with people in the workplace in his parish in Oakland. It has been very difficult to find people who will reflect on the work experience and see it as anything other than an individual effort. A corporate approach seems to make little sense to them.

MR. TOZZI: The workplace was a common topic of reflection in a study group in which my wife and I took part. So it is of interest to people.

SR. GARLAND: Many of the lay ministry training programs in the country are modeled on the priesthood. The question arises whether the laity should receive training that responds to their own life situations, which would include the workplace.

PARTICIPANT: Fr. Murnion noted that some studies suggest most of the people who leave the Church do so for global reasons rather than dissatisfaction with the parish. This seems to contradict another study, a very important one done for Fr. Alvin Illig's evangelization office, which seemed to show that dropouts from the Church are people unhappy with the unkindness of their pastor. This is consistent with the finding of the Notre Dame study that parishioners want a pastor who is sensitive to them. Dr. Dean Hoge of The Catholic University of America, who is with us today, did that study. Isn't it true that dropouts do generally say they left because of the way they were treated by a particular priest?

DR. HOGE: As we all know, there is a huge dropping out from parish life, mostly in the teenage and college years. This is true of all Christian denominations. When you talk with these people, they often say unkind things about priests. Very often an authority conflict is involved; the priest didn't allow them to do what they wanted to do. But you only hear one side of the story, and it is hard to say what the truth of the matter is. To my mind, unhappiness with leadership is not a major cause of dropping out. The dropping out is so pervasive, it is absolutely everywhere.

FR. CRESPIN: Fr. Murnion, your closing remarks?

FR. MURNION: I know a very dedicated pastor who tells me that whenever he has a couple getting married, and one of them has not been active in the Church, he always asks why. The first response is often a complaint about a pastor. If my friend pushes the matter, the next response has to do with some teaching of the Church. If he pushes it a little more, he finds out that the person just got careless and dropped out and got into the habit of sleeping in on Sunday morning. It is interesting how consistent this pattern is.

I have nothing further to add by way of conclusion.

THE PARISH AT WORSHIP

SPEAKER

Dr. Mark Searle
Assistant Professor of Theology, University of Notre Dame

PANEL

Fr. Raymond B. Kemp
Secretary for Parish Life, Archdiocese of Washington

Sr. Sheila Browne, RSM
Director of Music Ministry, St. Kevin's Parish
Flushing, New York

Fr. Ronald J. Lewinski
Director of the Liturgy Training Center, Archdiocese of Chicago

Dr. Ralph Keifer
Professor of Liturgy, Catholic Theological Union

Msgr. Joseph M. Champlin
Vicar for Parish Life, Diocese of Syracuse

A celebrated nineteenth-century historian of the liturgy once remarked, "Because I am not a theologian, I can praise God with joy." In much the same spirit, I should preface my remarks by saying, "Because I am not a sociologist, I can praise God without counting heads." On the other hand, because I am a liturgist, I can rarely praise God without thinking of ways in which the liturgy could be improved.

I will offer three kinds of data that concern the liturgical and devotional lives of American Catholics who are registered parish members and the parish Masses they attend.

First, we will examine descriptions of 70 Masses celebrated in 36 parishes over a period of approximately ten weeks, from early October through early December 1983. The study assigned two observers to each parish, asking them to observe the principal Sunday Mass, plus one other where more than one Mass was celebrated each weekend. The result is 140 very full descriptions, 85 covering Sunday morning Masses and 55 covering Saturday evening Masses, celebrated in parishes of different sizes, in different regions of the United States, and in different settings ranging from the inner city to small towns.

Second, we will review what Catholic people—parishioners, pastors, professional parish workers, and volunteers—have to say about the pattern of their religious lives and their experience of the liturgy.

Last, rather tentatively, we will try to understand how American Catholics see Christianity and the Church. Many of us would like to think that the ongoing experience of regular liturgical participation forms people's religious imagination so that their understanding of God, Church, self, and world reflects the images and values conveyed by the Church's liturgy. Our data will allow us to consider whether such expectations are realistic.

Going to Mass on Sunday provides an opportunity for parishioners to meet one another and establish relationships with their fellow parishioners. Those who avail themselves of this opportunity tend to do so after Mass rather than before. At fewer than 10% of the Masses attended by our observers was there any sizeable gathering before the liturgy began, whereas in 67% of the cases people tended to tarry and chat afterwards. (Of course, one can point out that fully one-third of the time people simply dispersed and went their separate ways as soon as Mass was over.) Coffee and donuts were served after 18% of the Masses, and in 7% of the cases some form of adult education preceded or followed Mass.

The size, style, and beauty of the church building seem to have little impact on where people choose to go to Mass. Nevertheless, it is worth noting that in only one parish in five was the church filled to capacity at the main Mass, while in the same percentage of parishes the church was less than half-full at the best-attended Mass. Whether the size of the congregation makes a difference, and what kinds of difference it makes in people's experience of liturgy, remain to be explored.

We asked our observers to describe how people behaved as they waited for Mass to begin. Almost half of their reports noted people reading their parish bulletin. Only 5 of the 140 reports mentioned confessions being heard before Mass, while 84% mentioned people engaged in private prayer. At almost 10% of the Masses attended, people were chatting in church before Mass began, while in just over 30% of the cases there was some kind of musical rehearsal with the congregation. Twenty-four of the reports said that the priest or the servers were setting up for Mass as the people drifted in. Nearly 20% of the Masses began more than five minutes late.

What did these Catholics have in their hands at Mass? A clear favorite was the missalette, used at 76% of the Masses—principally *Today's Missal* and *We Celebrate*. Forty-six percent of the parishes appear to have invested in hymnals, including *Today's Missal* (16.6%), *We Celebrate* (11.6%), and *Worship II* (10%). Nearly 40% of parishes provided song-books of various kinds. *Glory and Praise,* vol. I, stands out; one in four of our parishes use it. Another 10% had their own parish collections, almost all of them compilations of contemporary folk music. While some music was part of most of the Masses attended, 13% offered no music or singing at all.

Practices often vary from Mass to Mass within the same parish: some have folk music, others hymnody, others no music at all. Of the Masses attended by our observers, Gregorian chant or chant-like music was reported in only 8 of 140 cases. In 18, polyphony was used, but never exclusively. Eight reports noted the use of gospel music, and French or Polish hymns were sung in scattered instances. The principal contemporary music, however, is clearly folk. Folk predominated at 46% of all Masses, while hymnody was dominant at 34%.

The reports yield an abundance of information on what was done, by whom, and how at these Masses. We shall be content here merely to highlight some of the more accessible and interesting items.

The present opening rites of the Roman Mass appear to be unpopular with a number of celebrants. In 30% of the Masses, the sign of the cross was omitted altogether, while in another 38% it was preceded by a greeting or some other opening remarks. Twenty-five reports indicate that the celebrant greeted the congregation with "Good morning" or "Good evening," while 30% of the Masses began with no introduction at all. A few opened with extensive greetings of various groups of people, the announcement of Mass intentions, references to the liturgy of the day, and so on. In 7% of the cases the penitential rite was omitted entirely; another 3% featured only the *Kyrie*. Among the options provided in the Sacramentary, option three, the *Kyrie*-litany, was the clear favorite (40%) over option one (the *Confiteor:* 28%) and option two (13%). The *Gloria* was recited at 65% of these Masses. It was more often omitted (21.4%) than sung (13.6%), though the fact that some of the last observations

(8.7%) took place on the first Sunday of Advent may account for the rather high rate of omission.

Lay ministers are clearly flourishing in our land. In only 10 of 140 reports did the celebrant or deacon do the first and second readings. The responsorial psalm has not met with quite the same success: in almost half the Masses observed, it was recited rather than sung. If there was music, its form varied greatly. The psalm might be read with a sung antiphon, or the psalm might be sung and the antiphon recited by the congregation, or both might be sung by the choir or a cantor, or any combination of the above. The gospel acclamation fared better, being sung at almost three-quarters of the Masses observed. The gospel procession has clearly not caught on. Fewer than 5% of the Masses had such a procession and in only three instances were lights carried.

The homily is another council mandate that has been taken seriously. In only two of the Masses was it omitted, and in only one case was it preached by a priest who came in for that specific purpose and then left. Thirty-eight of the reports mentioned the presence of an assisting deacon and in 12 of these instances the deacon delivered the homily. Still, the council's vision of a homily that would "break the bread of God's Word" is not yet entirely realized. While over 50% of the homilies were based on the readings, 22% made little or no mention of them at all.

As far as the parts following the homily are concerned, the prayers of the faithful were offered in almost all of the Masses, but the sung creed is nearly extinct. Only one sighting was reported.

Moving to the liturgy of the Eucharist, we can report that the offertory procession is in general use (only seven omissions), though the variations on what is brought in procession and by whom are enormous. At one Mass alone was incense used at the offertory. At six Masses the preface was sung, and at two the celebrant sang the whole eucharistic prayer. The congregation sang the *Sanctus* (57.1%) and the *Great Amen* (55.1%) at slightly more than half the Masses. The *Eucharistic Acclamation* was sung only a little less frequently (46%). Otherwise these texts were simply recited (*Sanctus,* 27%; *Eucharistic Acclamation,* 36%; *Great Amen,* 26%), were sung without congregational participation by the choir, or, in a few instances, were sung by the celebrant alone.

Lay ministers of communion abound, although they are not quite so strongly entrenched as lay readers. At 54 of the 70 Masses observed, laypeople assisted with the distribution of Holy Communion; at ten Masses, extra priests appeared to help out. Deacons, concelebrants, religious men and women, and even altar servers also functioned as ministers of communion.

The popes have been trying to restore the practice of frequent communion at least since the time of Pius X, but only recently have these efforts borne fruit. Our observers noted less than 70% of the congregation receiving communion at only five Masses. Even longer-standing has been the effort to convince priests to use hosts actually consecrated at the same Mass. This practice was followed at 19% of the Masses. At 16%, however, hosts for communion were still being brought exclusively from the tabernacle, while in the rest of the Masses hosts from both sources were used. Locally baked breads rather than hosts were distributed at five Masses.

Even though the number of people receiving communion has increased, communion under both species is not generally accepted. The chalice was not available to the laity at slightly more than half the Masses (54%). Moreover, where it was available, the number of those receiving from the cup was much smaller than the total going to communion. Only at 12 Masses did more than 70% of the congregation receive the cup. We noted no rite of sending communion to the sick at any of the Masses.

People tended to leave quickly once Mass was over. Only at one Mass did our researchers note that most of the congregation (over 70%) stayed behind for a time to pray. In more than half the cases, no one at all lingered to pray privately.

Clearly the liturgical reforms of Vatican II have been universally implemented, but in the letter rather than the spirit. It is taking time for the new liturgy to catch on. As we have just seen, many people do not receive from the cup, even when they have the chance. Furthermore, adoption of the new liturgy has not been an unmixed blessing. We note, for example, that frequent communion appears firmly established, but we also note that the quiet prayerfulness that used to follow the Mass appears to be in decline.

Our misgivings are strengthened by the evaluations we asked our observers to make regarding the quantity and quality of participation at various points in the Mass. They reported that in 48% of the Masses participation in the opening rites, which one might consider indicative of how the rest of the celebration is likely to go, ranged from mechanical to listless. About half the time, more than three-fourths of the congregation appeared to be joining in the spoken responses, and a slender 9 of 140 reports mentioned that a large majority of the people joined in the singing during the opening rites. During the eucharistic liturgy, the *Sanctus,* the *Acclamation* and the *Great Amen* engaged a sizeable majority of the congregation (over 70%) at only 28% of the Masses. Our observers detected no signs of boredom or restlessness at only 4 of 70 Masses, while at 12 of them the majority of those present showed signs of restlessness.

The relative enthusiasm of a congregation is notoriously difficult to assess objectively. People betray boredom through body language and in other ways, but much depends on where the observer is stationed and whether the people in the immediate vicinity are typical of the congregation as a whole. (We asked observers to take their places at different spots in the congregation and to compare their impressions afterwards.) Nevertheless, the reports confirm what most of us who sit regularly in the pews can see, and what the parishioners themselves frequently acknowledged, namely, that participation is not all it might be. Congregational participation is higher for the spoken responses and for the invariable parts of the rite, lower for sung parts and for parts, like the

Eucharistic Acclamation, that vary. (One should also note that support for sung participation leaves much to be desired. Thirteen percent of the Masses had no music at all; 51% had no organ accompaniment; 62% had no cantor; and 66% had no choir or music group to lead the congregation.) It is not surprising that American Catholics are unhappy with the musical aspects of their liturgy. As for our observers themselves, about one in five of the Masses they attended had a positive impact on them. Almost 50% of the time they found nothing to engage them.

As we have seen, parishes, even Masses in the same parish, differ considerably. Still, the cumulative picture that emerges from these reports is probably a fairly accurate reflection of the overall state of the liturgical life of American parishes and the way the liturgical renewal has been implemented. It provides a useful tool for pastoral liturgists to gauge what has been accomplished and what remains to be done. The picture can be sharpened still further if it is studied in conjunction with what parishioners themselves have to say about their liturgical and devotional lives. We now turn to these comments.

As we examine the laity's own report of their experience of liturgy in these 36 parishes, it is important to remember two things. First, the people who responded to our questionnaire are not entirely typical of the United States Catholic population as a whole. Our sample is drawn from Catholics who are registered in parishes. Over 71% of them claim to go to Mass every week, compared with a national level of Mass attendance of 44%. Second, the variety of liturgical styles available in most parishes means that, while people may live in the same parish and attend the same church, they may well have quite different liturgical experiences. (That is why it is more useful to speak, as we have so far, in terms of Masses observed rather than parishes visited.) Some of our respondents asserted that communion from the cup was not practiced in their parish, or that there were no women ministers of communion, or even that there was no sung liturgy, when in fact these features did appear at one or another Mass. Because of the vagaries of liturgical practice and differing levels of congregational participation, it may be that the situation is, in some particular instances, better than the general figures would suggest. On the other hand, because of the difference between core Catholics and the Catholic population at large, the general picture that emerges concerning Catholic practices and attitudes is certainly more optimistic than would have been the case had we sampled Catholics at large.

Let us begin by examining the broad devotional life of the Catholics in our sample. Not only do our respondents attend Sunday Mass with great regularity, but almost 10% of them regularly attend one or more weekday Masses. Over 61% pray privately every day and almost 8% engage in some form of family prayer other than grace at meals. (Sixty percent offer grace at least once a week.) These parishioners also read the Bible: 5% of them every day, 67% from time to time alone, and 27% from time to time with others. This is an impressive record for a people to whom the Bible has traditionally been regarded as something of a closed book. Not surprisingly, Catholics in the South and along the mid-Atlantic Coast are somewhat more likely than Catholics elsewhere to be readers of the Scriptures.

While these core Catholics appear to have a fairly solid prayer life, traditional Catholic devotions are rather clearly in decline among them. Thus, 46% of our respondents never attend benediction; 61% never join in the public recitation of the rosary; over 76% never go to a novena; and 44% never make the stations of the cross. Age, of course, is a significant factor here. The median age at which people go above or below the average for engaging in devotional practices such as these is 50. To illustrate: 25% of those aged 70 and over and 35% of those in their 50s and 60s never make the stations of the cross, while 44% of those in their 40s, 51% of those in their 30s, and 48% of those under 30 never do so.

Is this the result of conciliar influence on younger people, or does it reflect the religious life cycle? It may well be largely a matter of the life cycle, since the same sort of curve appears when we examine the figures for participation in communal penance services. Only 31% of people over 70 said they never took part in penance services, as compared with 50% of those under 40 and nearly 60% of those under 30. So, we are not simply seeing older Catholics clinging to older devotional practices and younger people embracing new forms of devotion. Devotions, it seems, are the prerogative of older people, and it is too early to say whether postconciliar Catholics will become more devotion-oriented as they age.

On the other hand, there are some indications that postconciliar emphases have made themselves felt in ways that distinguish those who grew up before the council from those who grew up during and after it. One such indication is frequency of reception of communion. As the following table shows, older people go to Mass and receive communion more frequently than younger people, but those under 50, and especially those under 40, are less likely to abstain from receiving communion than their elders.

Age Groups:	Under 30	30–39	40–49	50–69	Over 70
Weekly Mass	50%	61%	72%	79.5%	79%
Weekly Communion	41%	52%	60%	65%	65%

If one aim of the liturgical renewal was to restore the connection between attending Mass and receiving communion, another was to focus Catholic prayer life more on God and Christ and less on Mary and the saints. Here again, younger parishioners seem to have been more responsive to the change in emphasis. While older Catholics are more likely to engage in daily prayer than younger Catholics (74% of those over 70 pray daily compared with 52% of those under 30), when we asked the parishioners to whom they address their prayers, a marked distinction between the generations appeared, as the table shows.

Age Groups:	Under 30	30–39	40–49	50–69	Over 70
God/Christ only	57%	56%	43%	30%	23%
God/Christ/Mary	25%	21%	31%	29%	25%
God/Christ/Mary/Saints	18%	16%	19%	30%	38%
Mary/Saints only	—	6%	6%	11%	14%

Here is evidence of a remarkable shift in devotional patterns that is much more likely to reflect the changing ethos of Catholicism in this country than merely to be an epiphenomenon of the religious life cycle. Though some might feel nervous about the decline in devotion to the saints and, to a lesser degree, to Mary, the clear trend is toward a more theocentric and Christocentric prayer life, consonant with the thrust of Vatican II's Constitution on the Liturgy and the subsequent reforms of the liturgy and calendar.

One area of religious practice where changes have occurred that the council did not intend is penance. The move from a single form of private confession, whose statistics were easily and accurately kept, to three sacramental rites of reconciliation plus nonsacramental penance services complicates the researcher's job. But we can rely on what people tell us at least as regards confession. They tell us that 26% of core Catholics never go to confession and only 6% go once a month or more. As one might expect, age is a significant factor here, too. Whereas 90% of people over 70 go to confession at least from time to time, only 62% of those under 30 do so. Monthly confession is the rule for 11% of those over 70, 8% of those in their 50s and 60s, 4% of those in their 30s and 40s, and 2% of those under 30. Once again, the curve probably represents the life cycle; it is arguable whether the decline in confessional practice has been greater among the young than among the old.

There is not much evidence that this decline in the frequency of confession is directly related to the introduction of communal liturgies of penance and reconciliation, nor that these latter are replacing confession. Once again, it is the elderly who are more likely to participate in penance services: nearly 60% of parishioners under 30 say they never take part in public penance services, while only 20% of those over 70 say the same. Because of major differences in the availability of communal penance services from parish to parish, the data need to be analyzed rather carefully. However, the fact that nearly half of our parishioners said they both go to confession and take part in penance services (43%), while a small percentage (7%) only take part in penance services and never go to confession, seems to suggest that fears that public penance will undermine private confession are probably exaggerated.

Nevertheless, the drop in the frequency of confession and the avoidance even by core Catholics of any form of the sacrament are phenomena that cry out for pastoral evaluation. It is tempting to blame these phenomena on a loss of the sense of sin among American Catholics and to advocate more attention to moral matters in the pulpit and in the classroom. Sin, however, is always a matter of definition. The problem may lie not in a widespread lack of moral sensitivity—though that is always arguable—but in the lack of agreement about what is permissible and what is not, a lack of strong consensus about the boundary between being in good standing as a Catholic and not being in good standing.

While more needs to be done with our data on Catholic self-definition, one example may suffice to show that inquiry into this definition holds promise. We asked our respondents about a number of patterns of behavior that might be considered to identify a person as an unfaithful Catholic, to put him or her outside the Church. These behaviors included habitually missing Mass, living together without benefit of marriage, marrying outside the Church, opposing racial integration, opposing nuclear disarmament, practicing homosexuality, and committing major or minor crimes. Of all these, the clearest disciplinary rule and most traditional "boundary setter" is probably Mass attendance. Yet, 46% of our respondents—core Catholics—thought that if a person habitually misses Mass he or she can still be considered "a true Catholic." In suburban parishes, this tolerance of what used to be labelled delinquency rises to 53%. A single finding is obviously not enough to prove anything. It may be worth asking, however, whether the decline in the practice of confession reflects the general cultural supposition that we must all be free to make up our own minds. To the extent that Catholics accept such an axiom without qualification, any sense of collective identity, or of boundaries between outside and inside, belonging and not belonging, will necessarily be eroded.

When we asked how moral decisions are to be made, nearly half our respondents claimed to believe that God has given very clear, detailed rules to apply. Almost the same number believes that God has given us ideals to strive for rather than rules to obey, or that God has given us rules but we ourselves must decide how to apply them. In any case, when we asked people to apply what they thought were the rules to test cases, wide disparities of judgment emerged. As I say, further analysis is needed. One may suggest, however, that the practice of sacramental penance, implying forgiveness by and reconciliation with the Church, is hardly likely to flourish in any of its forms if a strong sense of ecclesial identity is lacking. If the mediation of the Church can be ignored in the definition of our religious identity and standing, its mediation can equally well be dispensed with in healing our relationship with God.

Paradoxically, part of the responsibility for the decline in the practice of sacramental penance may rest with preachers and teachers who put much emphasis on interiority and little on ecclesial identity and vocation. By playing down the role of penance as reconciliation with the Church, by emphasizing natural law morality, by asserting the primacy of individual confession, we may in fact be abetting the individualism of our culture to undermine the public, social, and sacramental character of the Catholic tradition. This is admittedly hypothetical.

Let us glance at how the by now not-so-new liturgy is appreciated by our parishioners. Liturgists tend to view the celebration of the liturgy as central to the life of the Church and hence of the parish, and they expect the quality of liturgical participation to be a major factor in how enthusiastically people identify with their parish. In actual fact, while 20% of the people in our survey regularly attend Mass in a parish other than their own, of this 20% only 3% (5% in the suburbs) mentioned the quality of the liturgy as a reason for switching. As a motivation, this lags well behind considerations of time (38%) and place (5.5%). Asked about their own parish, 56% said they attend that church simply because they reside within its territory. Only 7% (11% in the suburbs) cited style of worship as their parish's primary attraction. While this rating is higher than that for quality of preaching (4%) and attachment to the church building (3%), it falls far short of that for quality of pastoral care (17%) and friendliness of the parishioners (14%). We must conclude that liturgical style and the quality of the celebration are not major factors in determining where core Catholics worship. Not many people "shop around" for good liturgy, perhaps because good liturgy is hard to find, perhaps because Catholics are not terribly discriminating where liturgy is concerned.

It would be unfair to say, however, that our parishioners are entirely uncritical of what they see and hear on Sunday. They do notice and react to changes. We found relatively little opposition to the new liturgy as such. What opposition there is, moreover, is not confined to a particular age group or a particular region of the country, although parishioners in the Midwest registered more dissatisfaction than those in other regions, and people in the Mountain States were the most enthusiastic about what has been happening. Rather than resting content with a generic question about whether people like or dislike the liturgy, we tried to assess their reactions to different aspects of it. Regarding each element, we asked people whether they were happy that it had been added, whether they would prefer it were omitted, or whether they had no strong opinion one way or the other.

As might have been anticipated, there is some disquiet about lay ministers of communion. Twenty percent of all respondents would prefer not to have women ministering communion, and 17% do not like male lay ministers either. Less than half were entirely happy about the advent of lay ministers of communion (39% for women ministers, 43% for men); the rest did not mind.

As we saw above, laypeople had no part in distributing communion at 23% of the Masses we observed. Yet only 6% of parishioners claimed that laymen did not distribute communion in their parish, and only 10% said there were no women ministers in their parish. Similarly, the cup was withheld from the laity at 52% of the Masses our observers attended, but less than a quarter of the respondents said that communion from the cup was unavailable in their parish. These discrepancies show that practice is by no means uniform at all Masses in a given parish. At some, apparently, lay ministers of communion are used and communion is given under both species, while neither practice applies at other Masses. Perhaps the level of parishioner dissatisfaction with these practices is linked to the incompleteness of their implementation, which may in turn reflect a lack of conviction among parish leadership as to their importance.

It is no great secret that the cup has been extended to the laity at Sunday Mass only with a great deal of official hesitation. This reluctance militates against any effective catechesis; the lack of catechesis could be the reason why 15% of the parishioners would prefer that the cup not be available, while another 32% are indifferent to whether it is or not. Our observers noted that only in 17% of the Masses did the majority of the congregation (over 70%) receive communion from the cup. If we are convinced of the symbolic-sacramental value of communion under both kinds, there is clearly a major catechetical job to be done.

In contrast, communion in the hand and the kiss of peace now seem well-rooted in Catholic ritual. There is still some residual dislike of these practices—11% of parishioners wish communion in the hand could be discontinued, and 13% would like to drop the kiss of peace—but 55% declare themselves happy with the former and just over 61% with the latter. (People are rather more likely to be either for or against the kiss of peace than for or against communion in the hand, presumably because receiving communion is a matter of personal choice, while the kiss of peace is a social gesture demanding interaction.)

We asked parishioners to rate the quality of their parish liturgy in terms of its music, singing, prayers, readings, and ritual performance. There was little dissatisfaction with the readings and prayers (under 3% each), but 17% of the respondents said that the ritual in general was unsatisfactory or in need of improvement. Music seems to present the most widespread problem. Only 63% were satisfied with the quality of music in their parish, and only 60% were happy with the singing. These people do not want singing eliminated altogether; only 4% of our population took that position. So the overwhelming majority is glad to have some music, but 40% are dissatisfied with what is sung and how it is sung. This dissatisfaction runs as high as 50%, on average, in rural parishes and as low as 29% in suburban parishes. The statistical spread is not surprising considering that smaller and especially rural parishes lack the resources available to larger, wealthier suburban parishes. Interestingly, the age factor does not seem to make much difference, except that those under 30 are more likely to be critical both of the quality of the music and of the singing. This subject bears closer scrutiny.

If we combine what our observers saw in the parishes with parishioners' comments on contemporary liturgical practice, we can offer some preliminary conclusions. The connection between attending Mass and receiving communion now seems well established, though communion from the cup and communion with hosts consecrated at the same Mass are not yet the rule. The proper subordination of devotions to the liturgical prayer of the Church seems to be widely accepted. (Whether the sharp decline in such devotional exercises as benediction and the stations of the cross is altogether desirable remains a matter for pastoral judgment, however.) Finally, the level and quality of liturgical participation in our congregations seem to call for careful attention, particularly as regards music.

Reflection on the data concerning sacramental penance raises a question profound in its implications and difficult to answer. This question has to do with how well our respondents have assimilated the declared meaning and purpose of liturgical reform: a renewed sense of ecclesial identity.

Certainly it is impossible to talk about the liturgical life of American Catholics today without assessing present realities in the light of conciliar expectations and vice versa. The Second Vatican Council, especially as regards the liturgy, did not simply introduce reforms; it also gave a rationale for them. The reforms themselves may be considered secondary to a larger change of understanding that was the council's goal. The Constitution on the Liturgy makes it quite clear that liturgical reform is not an end in itself, but rather a means to church renewal. In the familiar phrases of the Constitution's opening paragraph, the council aimed "to impart an ever-increasing vigor to the Christian life of the faithful; to adapt more closely to the needs of our age those institutions which are subject to change; to foster whatever can provide union among all who believe in Christ; to strengthen whatever can help to call mankind into the Church's fold."

It was clearly the hope of the leaders of the liturgical movement, a hope shared by the bishops of Vatican II, that a renewed liturgy would result in a renewed sense of Church. In Pius X's much-touted phrase, "the liturgy of the Church is the source of the authentic Christian spirit." Thus, a liturgy which was "returned to the people" might be expected to bring about a shift among Catholics everywhere from an individualistic conception of their Christian identity to an understanding of the Church as a single Body of which we are all members. It is becoming clear that if the liturgy is indeed capable of such influence, the shift in attitude will be slow and uneven.

Regrettably, we have no studies of "the Catholic imagination" as it existed on the eve of the council with which to compare the findings of the parish study. Furthermore, it is difficult to identify with complete confidence attitudes and motivations that can be characterized as clearly individualistic or communitarian. One begins by isolating a number of characteristics associated with these two viewpoints and attempts to develop a profile for each against which people's responses can be measured. The work of developing this profile based on the data contained in the study is still in process. Here we can only examine certain selected findings and suggest the direction in which they seem to point.

When we asked people to identify the single most important reason why they attend Mass, we found that both authority and the attractions of liturgical participation play a far less prominent role than might be expected. Only 6% of core Catholics said their reason for going to Mass is that the Church requires them to do so. Age is significant here: nearly 8% of those over 50 gave duty as their main reason, compared with less than 2% of those under 30. Interestingly, although parish staffs and pastors are generally quite accurate in their perceptions of what their parishioners think, in this instance they were wide of the mark. Twenty-three percent of pastors and 19% of parish staff personnel gave duty as the main reason their parishioners attend Mass. It may well be that these leaders were thinking of parishioners as a whole rather than just the core Catholics we sampled. They may also have been noticing, as our observers did, that Catholics respond rather apathetically to the call to more active participation in the rite, and have drawn the mistaken conclusion that most of their flock does not really want to be there.

One could rejoice at the wane of legalism, at least among core Catholics, if one could be sure that a positive conviction about belonging to the Church (which the Sunday Mass obligation is meant to foster) were on the rise. But it is not at all clear that this is the case. Just under 5% said they went to Mass because they enjoy being with others—a clearly "horizontal" motive—and another 28% said they went because they enjoy taking part in the liturgy. The most popular reason (37%) was the more private one of meditating and being with God.

Neither duty nor the feeling of being with God are necessarily indicators of an individualistic or pre-Vatican II mindset. They have to be considered along with other indicators. Almost the same number of people said that they go to Mass to hear the Word of God as said that they go to receive Holy Communion (20% each), which may indicate that the conciliar reforms have had some effect. Attention to the Word of God was slightly stronger in the mid-Atlantic States than elsewhere and was markedly stronger among black Catholics (28.5%). Receiving communion was the main motivation of 38% of Catholics over 70, but of only 7% of Catholics under 30.

In a more direct attempt to discover the degree to which American Catholics are influenced by the communitarianism of the liturgy on the one hand and by individualism on the other, we asked our respondents to choose from among five models the one most closely corresponding to the way they envisage their relationship to the Church, to God, and to Christ. The Arian model of Christ as simply a great man elicited minimal response. Parishioners were fairly equally divided among the other four. Of these, the first two are clearly individualistic. The first situates Jesus and his redemptive work in the past; each of us now has direct and individual access to God (22%). The second model restores the continuing mediatorship of Christ, but still makes access to God an individual matter (26%). Taken together, these one-to-one conceptions of our relationship to God, which tend to bypass the Church, commanded the assent of nearly half our core Catholics (48%).

The third model was that of the hierarchical, institutional Church to which Christ is present and which teaches and sanctifies us. This claimed 22% of the responses. The Mystical Body image, the fourth, claimed 23%. It seems fair to say that, if the Mystical Body model comes closest to symbolizing the organic unity of the baptized which the liturgy presupposes and should promote, then only a minority of churchgoers have the kind of vision which is congruent with the spirit of the liturgy. Half have individualistic conceptions of their membership in the Church quite at odds with this spirit. Parish staff display a different pattern. Only 32% have individualistic conceptions, and 30% accept the Mystical Body image. The Mystical Body was the preferred image of 50% of the pastors; just under 13% had individualistic concepts. The institutional model of the Church as teacher and sanctifier was most popular among parish staffs (tied with the Mystical Body at 30%) and least popular among parish volunteers (16%).

Another possible indicator of the strength of individualism is the answers people gave when asked how they pray during the liturgy. Very few people claimed to say their own prayers exclusively during the Mass (less than 4%) and only .2% say they do not pray at all. Here again the sense of community seems to be stronger among the professionals than the laity. Forty-six percent of the laity say they pray exclusively with the congregation, while 50% say they pray with the congregation but also say their own prayers. Among parish staffs, 90% pray exclusively with the congregation; only 9% say they also say their own prayers.

What of liturgy as a source of religious experience? Fifty-six percent of the laity in our study claimed to have had what they identified as a "religious experience" at some time in their lives. Only 6.5%, however, said this experience occurred in a liturgical context, while another 1.4% mentioned baptism explicitly as the occasion. Only 3 of 35 pastors claiming a religious experience said it happened during the liturgy, while one said he had had such an experience at baptism. Six percent of staff personnel had had a religious experience at liturgy, and another 2.5% mentioned baptism. (The references to baptism, though statistically minimal, are nevertheless interesting, especially since these questions were open-ended.)

Religious experiences were described by our respondents as rare moments of unusual closeness to God marked by such feelings as peace, joy, and trust. The more mundane life of Catholics is also characterized by a definite, if undramatic, awareness of the presence of God, a presence more likely to be noticed in regularly recurring situations or fixed times of devotion. We asked people to identify the contexts in which, as a rule, they feel closest to God. Here the liturgical-sacramental element in Catholic life comes more strikingly to the fore. Sixty-eight percent said they felt extremely close to God in receiving communion and 48% said the same of other sacramental moments, such as absolution or anointing. Sixty-two percent identified private prayer times as occasions of greatest intimacy. About half that number said they felt very close to God in gathering with the congregation for the liturgy, while 28% said the same of praying and chanting the liturgy. These figures are slightly higher for volunteer workers, but, as might be expected, the clergy are most likely to identify the liturgy as a setting where they feel close to God. More specifically, 40% felt this closeness in gathering with the congregation, 31% in praying the liturgy, and 49% in receiving communion. (By way of comparison, 60% reported feeling close to God during private prayer.)

When we asked how Catholics understand the "economy" of the Christian life (that is, what problem Christianity deals with, how it deals with this problem, and what the outcome is envisaged as being), differences between clergy and laity became more marked. Roughly the same percentage of both groups (17% of clergy, 15% of laity) tied the sacraments into this economy. Remarkably, for a majority of Catholics, the path to salvation lies not so much through the sacraments as through trust in God's forgiveness. On the other hand, the laity are clearly more likely (20% to 3%) than their pastors to see salvation in terms of winning God's favor by doing good works. They are also more likely to see salvation itself as consisting in life with God in heaven after death; 44% of the laity espouse this view as against 26% of the clergy. Thirty-three percent of the pastors tend to see salvation in terms of establishing peace and harmony (a this-worldly, public interpretation), while 30% of staff people take the more personal, though still this-worldly, view that salvation consists in finding meaning and happiness in one's earthly life. These findings suggest that those who have more invested in the Church—clergy and professional staff—are inclined to hope their investment will pay dividends here below. They may conceive of such dividends as social and public (the renewal of the face of the earth) or individual (personal satisfaction). On the contrary, "ordinary" Catholics, less involved with internal church affairs and more with the secular realm, are inclined to put their hopes in a life after death and do not expect religion to make much immediate difference in their lives or in the life of the world.

We began this last section by asking whether Catholics share a strong sense of being organic members of the Body of Christ, as the liturgy seems to suppose. By and large, one would have to say "no." Only a minority explicitly identify with the Body of Christ image or see the sacramental celebrations of the Church as integral to the path to salvation. The data on feeling close to God, on the motivations for attending Mass, and on how people pray at liturgy are ambivalent and need further examination. Still, there is enough evidence to say that, while liturgical reforms have been put in place, the kinds of understanding they were intended to promote are by no means universal. One must be concerned, from a pastoral and liturgical perspective, that the radical individualism of our culture is more effective than liturgy and tradition in shaping the imaginations of Catholic people and influencing their behavior. There may not be much that can be done directly to challenge and correct such attitudes. However, if those with pastoral responsibility see the influence of culture as a major pastoral problem, they may at least be able to avoid aggravating it themselves.

These considerations strongly suggest the need to evaluate the findings of the Notre Dame study from a theological and pastoral point of view. Our findings, liturgical and otherwise, should prompt reflection rather than immediate action. The Christian Gospel and the Catholic tradition are too precious to allow our culture to absorb them. The only safeguard against such a trend is hard-nosed theological and pastoral reflection, to which I now invite my colleagues.

PANEL DISCUSSION

DR. BUTLER: To introduce our presenter and the members of the panel who will react to his talk, I will turn the microphone over to Fr. Raymond Kemp, secretary for parish life of the Archdiocese of Washington. Fr. Kemp is responsible for networking all the parish staffs and lay leaders of the archdiocese and is one of the most influential clergymen in Washington. In addition to his work locally, Fr. Kemp is one of the founders of the North American Forum on the Catechumenate.

FR. KEMP: Our panel has a fine speaker to which to respond. Mark Searle holds his doctorate from Trier, Germany. He taught liturgy and sacramental theology in Canterbury, England, and was at the Notre Dame Center for Pastoral Liturgy for some time before moving to the university's theology department two years ago. Dr. Searle and I have shared a number of platforms, going around the country discussing sacramental theology and conversion and the catechumenate. He is a thinker. He raises questions. He is the author of five books and countless essays, collections, and other publications. Those who listen to liturgists make it their business to find out what Mark Searle is saying, and he has certainly given us food for thought today.

Our first panelist is Sr. Sheila Browne, who was involved in Catholic education before becoming a full-time pastoral minister ten years ago. Sr. Browne holds degrees in music from Manhattanville College and from Queens College of the City University of New York, as well as a degree in liturgy from Notre Dame. She also writes book reviews for Fr. Murnion's new publication, *Church,* and bears diverse responsibilities in her position as pastoral minister at St. Kevin's Parish in Flushing, New York.

SR. BROWNE: I am curious about that point in Dr. Searle's talk where he considers liturgy as the occasion of religious experience. Apparently, the data show that only a small percentage of staff and laity had a religious experience in the celebration of the liturgy, but that a very small but significant group of people said gratuitously that this experience occurred in the celebration of the sacrament of baptism. I would ask Dr. Searle and those responsible for the further interpretation of the data whether these were adult or infant baptisms. What kind of preparation program was involved? If they were adult baptisms, then we can hope that they were preceded by a catechumenate of some length, during which time not only the candidates for the sacrament but also the staff involved undergo a certain catechesis together. If they were infant baptisms, what process did the parents, sponsors, parish staff, and sponsoring group in the parish go through? What kind of catechesis was carried out?

I think we should think about the kind of preparation program that can help people see the sacraments as integral to one's life. The study shows that the celebration of the sacraments and the celebration of liturgy are not on the cutting edge. What part can sacramental programs play in making them part of the economy of the Christian life?

The greater part of my reflections have to do with music. I have spent many years working with music in school and in church. I am disturbed at some of the study's findings. Seeing facts in black and white is a lot harder to take than surmising them from watching and listening to people.

I observe a great lack of conviction of the importance of music in the life of the Church. Many still see music as an unnecessary icing on the cake: the people in the pews who say they cannot or will not or just do not sing; musicmakers who do not do their homework, who are not good at their art, who are not good at their ministry, who bore us; and priests and deacons who say, "Let's sing only one verse of this hymn," or "Let's do only one verse of the responsorial psalm. Let's get in and get out." Priests who do not see the importance of music in liturgical celebration tend to take a minimalistic approach. It is the musical equivalent of the "three drops" theory of baptism or the "a dab will do you" theology of the anointing at confirmation. I think we need to reflect on the real liturgical function of hymns in our celebrations.

Who gets to say and do the good things at Mass? It is usually the priest. The lay lector will proclaim the Good News for the first two readings, but the priest says the eucharistic prayer and so on. Those of us in the pews say a few amens, and we get to sing. When we sing hymns, we sing the faith of the Church. I don't think enough of us realize this. The function of hymns is to put on the lips of the faithful what we believe. Whether it be the traditional hymn "Jesus Christ has Risen Today," which we sing at Easter, whether it be John Foley's "One Bread, One Body" or Michael Joncas' very beautiful communion song "When We Eat This Bread and Drink This Cup, We Proclaim Your Death until You Come," what a hymn does is put on the lips of the faithful the belief of the Church. It gives us a language and a vocabulary with which to express our faith. It is a much shorter distance from my lips to my heart than from the priest's lips to my heart.

I am reminded of Lee Mitchell's remark that you rarely hear a person leaving Mass humming the homily. The effect of music is pervasive and its pastoral dimensions deserve serious consideration. People in my parish say they find themselves singing something while doing their housework and suddenly realize it is the responsorial psalm from Sunday. One mother told me in an amazed tone that she heard her kids playing in the backyard and singing "We Have Put on Christ, in Him We Have Been Baptized."

I repeat, music is pervasive. These short refrains, repeated often through the year, can invade our subconscious and rise unbidden to our lips at any time. Thus, the sung prayer of the Church remains with us.

We all like old friends—that is, we like familiarity in the music we sing. The preponderance of good new music in the Church today makes some musicians forget the wisdom of the liturgical principle of invariability. We need to learn the new but must not abandon the old and familiar. The organ can be struck with lightning, the organist can be out of town, the song leader might have laryngitis, but we know that if the *Sanctus,* the *Amen,* and the *Eucharistic Acclamation* have been sung every week, the congregation will sing them well. How many of us were really very pleased and happy when we sang "Come Holy Ghost" last Sunday on the feast of Pentecost? It was as if an old friend had come back for a while.

One of the points from Dr. Leege's paper that we should bear in mind is the middle-class status of our Catholic people. They have experienced listening to the philharmonic at symphony hall or at home on a compact disk and quadraphonic sound system. They come to church and are shocked at the sounds they hear coming from the organist or the folk ensemble. Where are we to find fine pastoral musicians? Are they only a dream and not a hope?

The Pius X School of Liturgical Music at Manhattanville, which trained music leaders in this country in the 1930s, 1940s, and 1950s, is gone and nothing has taken its place. The Juilliard School and Indiana University's music department will not supply us with good liturgical organists. They will give us marvelous concert musicians, but none who will assume responsibility for liturgical music in the Church.

Some dioceses have begun training programs, certification programs, for music ministers. Catholic colleges and universities should be inaugurating departments or at least offering degrees in liturgical music, as do Notre Dame and The Catholic University of America. In this way, the seeds of musicianship and the fun of singing and participation will be planted in children in our Catholic schools and religious education programs. Further, we need pastors with the vision to hire and adequately pay qualified full-time pastoral musicians who will stay in the parish for some time and who, by their musicianship, their artistry, and their compassion will become real ministers to the people, so that the Church can sing its prayer.

FR. KEMP: Our next panelist is Fr. Ronald Lewinski, director of the Liturgy Training Center in the Archdiocese of Chicago. I have known

Fr. Lewinski for several years. He pioneered the development of the catechumenate in this country and is the author of a guide for sponsors in welcoming the new Catholic. He also shaped the publication called *The Chicago Catechumenate*.

FR. LEWINSKI: To take up Sr. Browne's point, I recently attended a meeting of cathedral musicians. One of their great concerns is that, even as more pastors begin to see the need for good professional liturgical musicians, there are not enough available. I'm afraid I don't see much hope for change in the near future.

Again, piggybacking a bit on what Sr. Browne was saying, we hear an awful lot these days about abuses in the liturgy. This talk usually refers to excesses. We should be just as concerned about the abuses of minimalism, but one hears few complaints about that.

Like music, environment and art in the liturgy deserve attention. Even though the study says that people are not necessarily attracted to a particular building for worship because of how it looks, that building still has an effect on how people worship and how they see themselves as a worshiping congregation. A priest who attended one of our workshops remarked that it was too bad his people would never be able to experience the liturgy we had celebrated the night before. When we asked why, he said, "Well, our church just isn't designed that way." Should we allow the bricks and mortar to shape how we worship? Or should our spiritual life shape the buildings we worship in?

When we talk about environment and art, it is not just a matter of interior decorating for liturgical space, choosing colors, and so on. We must ask whether we are putting new wine into old wineskins, whether we can really celebrate some of the new rites in an environment that often visually and physically reinforces a spirituality from another era. That is a very difficult question, I think.

While the study speaks of liturgical ministers, it has little to say about the presider. It certainly seems to me that the quality of the presiding plays a significant role in the total effect of the liturgy on the assembly. I am not referring only to how well the priest executes the liturgy but also, and more important, to his spirituality as he celebrates it. If the priest's spirituality derives from another era, it bleeds through and undercuts the effect of the liturgy. I think dioceses have yet to address this problem satisfactorily.

Finally, while we have all kinds of books and workshops on teaching people to pray, I have yet to see books or workshops aimed at helping people pray the liturgy. How do we develop liturgical spirituality in our people? We seem to presume that people will automatically catch liturgical spirituality. I am not at all sure that will happen.

FR. KEMP: Dr. Ralph Keifer is professor of liturgy at the Catholic Theological Union in Chicago. He is a graduate of Providence College, with a doctorate from Notre Dame, and he asked me to stress to you that he is a layperson. Dr. Keifer's two books are *The Mass in Time of Doubt,* from the National Association of Pastoral Musicians, and *Blessed and Broken.*

DR. KEIFER: I find certain things in the Notre Dame study striking. Roman Catholicism in this country seems to have undergone a thorough Americanization of its ethos. As far as the liturgical data are concerned, I believe that liturgists have had vastly inflated expectations of what liturgical change would do for people. I am inclined to suspect, after hearing the data from this study, that liturgical reform has been appropriated not so much as revitalization but as fashion. People bring to the liturgy all sorts of alien presuppositions and perspectives that gravely affect it. Take, for example, the high level of religious individualism that Dr. Searle noted.

Too little of our discourse on liturgy in the last 20 years has focused on the context in which liturgy takes place. Far more attention needs to be paid to the fact that a vital liturgical life, while it may center on what happens in church, happens at home and in the public square as well. The context of liturgical celebration is a web of domestic practices and public practice. I am somewhat distressed that the study asked no questions about either of those.

Reception of the Eucharist, for instance, seems to be turning into a merely respectable practice. Everybody who is a participant in parish life goes to communion and people who are not full communicants are—or seemed to be in terms of the study—cut off from that parochial life. In the past, fringe people could pray with the Church because the Church existed within a whole welter of public and domestic practices. I suggest we need to look at the context of liturgy. Our liturgies have become inculturated in such a way that they are not really liturgies at all, but rather church services.

FR. KEMP: Our final speaker really needs no introduction. Msgr. Joseph Champlin is probably the single most influential popularizer of the reformed liturgies of the Second Vatican Council, not only in the United States but also in other English-speaking countries. He has written many articles, besides a series of handbooks that helps people prepare for baptism, marriage, and even death. At key moments Msgr. Champlin is there.

MSGR. CHAMPLIN: My interest in the study lies in its implications for the future. What do the data say to us regarding the next few years, even the next few decades? I have been working for liturgical renewal in this country for almost 35 years. Over and over I have said that the most difficult challenge we face is moving our people from an exclusive focus on "I," a vertical orientation in prayer and worship, to a more inclusive sense that the liturgy is also "we," community oriented. The present study shows that this remains a problem. I don't think it is a cause for despair or discouragement; 20 years are a drop in the bucket as far as the history of the Church is concerned. Getting people to change their ingrained attitude is going to take time.

Speaking to both clergy and laity over the last six months or so, I get the impression that we may have to go back to the basics. I was reminded of this by Fr. Lewinski's remark that we haven't really trained people to pray the liturgy. People are reacting to things I said 20 years ago, as though they never heard them before. I see a basic reeducation of people as a necessity.

In a survey conducted, I believe, by the Federation of Diocesan Liturgical Commissions on how people evaluate their parish liturgies, the criteria were preaching, music, and the presider. The data from the Notre Dame study on the low value people ascribe to preaching surprise me. I would like to see this subject pursued. My own impression is that the ordinary person judges how the parish is going very much in terms of the homily.

I am concerned about the future. It is interesting that the staff and the clergy have a here-and-now view of salvation, in contrast to the laity's emphasis on life after death in heaven. This dichotomy—the difference between a this-worldly and an otherworldly theology—has enormous ramifications both for our liturgical stance and our pastoral practice.

My last point has to do with the findings showing that a priest's sensitivity makes a great deal of difference to parishioners. While individualism may be strong in our country, I think the lack of individual caring is even stronger. Our liturgy has to be concerned about that. Personally, I am a little concerned that people from opposite points on the theological spectrum both come up with the wrong pastoral conclusions. Those with an institutional pre-Vatican II approach to law are saying "no" to people and so are those with a post-Vatican II emphasis on the sacraments as signs of faith. I am a little uneasy about the lack of pastoral sensitivity in the present messy state of the Church.

FR. KEMP: Do the panelists have any comments to direct to one another? I will also entertain questions from the floor.

SR. BROWNE: I wonder if the here-and-now mentality has anything to do with another aspect of parish life: the striving as Christians to effect justice and peace. Does this finding indicate that more staff people are now aware of peace and justice issues and of the Church's goal to bring about peace and justice? Is this being revealed to the people in our parishes if they see salvation as having to do with the next world? It seems that we need to do a lot more in terms of encouraging works of peace and justice in our parishes.

FR. KEMP: When we started the RENEW program in the Archdiocese of Washington, we discovered that about 85% of the people on liturgy planning committees in the parishes had never planned liturgies before, had never had any experience with the liturgical process at all. If the tenure of a volunteer in the same job is about three years, it seems to me that we must be prepared to set up a regular training cycle for each new set of folks.

PARTICIPANT: My name is Peter Robinson. I wonder if, in your judgment, the trend toward small prayer and faith-sharing groups will create more "we-ism" as opposed to "I-ism" in the Church?

MSGR. CHAMPLIN: We have just finished our second session of RENEW in the Diocese of Syracuse. We have 20,000 people in 2,000 small groups. You can sense that unfolding of people caring about one another in a very small informal way. The result of RENEW is social justice, though the program is sugarcoated so people don't realize it.

FR. LEWINSKI: I am concerned that "we-ism" may come to mean simply that the small community is happy with itself, that it has lost sight of the connection between liturgy and social justice. The first liturgical reformers were also the people who were first involved with social justice. Somewhere along the line we lost that linkage; we need to recover the radical dimensions of what it means to break the bread.

FR. KEMP: It is important to make sure the small group is constantly relating back to the larger group, so that it remains part of the parish.

PARTICIPANT: I am Kathleen Hughes from Catholic Theological Union. My question focuses on the Rite of Christian Initiation of Adults; we may, as Dr. Keifer implied, expect too much of it. It has become virtually axiomatic for liturgists to say that if the RCIA were implemented in a parish, it would be a step toward the remaking of the Church. Primarily because it is process oriented and takes place in the midst of the community, the RCIA moves away totally from the individualistic model. Is there any indication in the data, first of all, that those parishes that did implement the RCIA are more communally oriented? Second, do you have any sense that the RCIA has not been implemented in a large number of parishes precisely because we are too individualistic?

DR. SEARLE: Our data show that about one-third of parishes have some form of RCIA. I say "some form" because it is always difficult to determine what the term means. I think we probably have enough information to get some sense of how wide an impact the RCIA is having in the parish, but the analysis is yet to be done.

PARTICIPANT: I am John Butler from Washington, D.C. What is the impact of the individualistic viewpoint on minorities, especially black and Hispanic? When we begin to examine the communal aspect of our gathering and worship and the action for social justice it should stimulate, there is much that could be said about influencing the dominant white middle class. The Notre Dame study seems to ignore this. Might someone want to comment?

DR. KEIFER: Interestingly, creative change in the liturgy has happened when the Church was identified in prayer with the cry of the poor. This pattern recurs in our history from the development of the cult of the saints in the fourth century, through the Franciscan revival of the thirteenth century, and into later devotional developments. In some ways the black community and the Hispanic community have retained a sense of extended family and living as community that the white middle class is losing. The preferential option for the poor needs to be realized; it is not the Church's choice, it is God's. Salvation comes from the poor. In terms of our liturgical life, we need a serious dialogue with minority people, because among them faith does rise to celebration and there is a sense of connection between prayer and justice. We have not yet developed the possibility of that kind of dialogue.

MSGR. CHAMPLIN: It is easier to motivate a white middle-class parishioner to direct charitable action than to systemic change for social justice.

SR. BROWNE: When I worked in Brooklyn, I used to worship occasionally at a black parish next to the Navy Yard. In the morning liturgy there would just be me and two or three women from the parish. At the prayer of the faithful, Mrs. Webster would pray for "my brother John, who is having a hard time giving up liquor" and "my sister Mary, who is having a hard time with her kids" and on and on through ten or twelve brothers and sisters. One day after Mass I said something to her about the large family she came from, and she said, "That is my building, not my family. Those are the brothers and sisters who live with me in the projects." This experience showed me that the feeling of community, in terms of praying for one another and worshiping together, is much stronger in black communities than in white communities.

DR. LEEGE: In the course of the study, we oversampled black Catholic parishes; 4 of the 36 were black. One can't assume that black Catholics have the overall characteristic of the whole black population in the United States. Two of the black parishes we studied were very upwardly mobile. Religion is quite individualistic in those parishes, and there is minimal concern for justice and peace issues. Further, when we matched similar white parishes with these two black parishes, we found income levels and education to be higher in the black parishes.

PARTICIPANT: I wonder how many of the 36 parishes studied offered such devotions as benediction, novenas, and the Sacred Heart Program, at least on an annual basis. These devotions went out the window with

Vatican II, it seems to me. When you ask how many people attend the old-time devotions, you must also ask how often they are made available. If the devotions are not offered, people cannot go.

I am not pessimistic about the Church. It requires strength to survive all these changes. Some of us are still struggling with Vatican I, much less Vatican II. Sister, you mentioned music, and music is great. But things get a little out of hand sometimes. For example, is it mandatory under church law that in every liturgy you sing one song that nobody knows?

SR. BROWNE: It helps to keep life interesting.

PARTICIPANT: Perhaps so. I have one more comment. Msgr. Champlin mentioned going back to the basics. There have been changes in our parish that are hard on older people. For example, the eucharistic ministers tend to be overused. If I remember rightly, the eucharistic minister was to help the priest where there was a shortage of priests. Well, we have plenty of priests, but we are stumbling over eucharistic ministers and commentators. Also, laity should not go out and minister to the sick; they are not to serve in place of the priest. When I want to see a priest, I want to see a priest, and I am speaking for a lot of older people. Laypeople cannot substitute for priests.

APPENDIX I

WELCOME

Joseph Cardinal Bernardin
Archbishop of Chicago

Mr. Fred L. Hofheinz
Lilly Endowment, Inc.

Dr. Francis J. Butler
President, FADICA

CONCLUSION

Rev. Philip J. Murnion
Director, National Pastoral Life Center

WELCOME

DR. BUTLER: On behalf of my colleagues and FADICA, it is a pleasure to open this symposium on the American Catholic Parish in Transition.

One of the most agreeable duties I have today is to welcome back our good friend and special guest, Cardinal Joseph Bernardin. Your Eminence, we obviously feel welcome in your archdiocese, for this is the second meeting we have conducted here within the last 18 months. The atmosphere here in the Church in Chicago is a tribute to your own warmth and gifted leadership.

Cardinal Bernardin has agreed to open our meeting with a few personal reflections on the subject matter, and then he will lead us in our opening prayer.

CARDINAL BERNARDIN: I am delighted that FADICA continues to choose Chicago as the place for its meetings. It is a real pleasure to welcome you here, both to the city and to the archdiocese, and I hope you will enjoy your stay with us.

It is my hope that your time in our midst will be grace-filled, as you pursue your concerns about parish life in the Church. I think that you have chosen your topic and your resource very well: the topic, "The American Catholic Parish in Transition," and the resource, "The Notre Dame Study of Catholic Parish Life."

As you traveled to Chicago for this meeting, you may have had an experience similar to the one that I often have when my plane circles the metropolitan area in its approach to O'Hare or Midway Airport. The beauty of Lake Michigan and Chicago's lake shore, I think, is especially awesome from the air. The tall skyscrapers of the downtown area stand out in contrast, while the expressways sprawl in all directions.

As the plane continues its descent, individual buildings begin to stand out in clearer relief. My eyes are often attracted to the many parishes that dot the landscape. There are 450 parishes here. Catholic churches are often easy to identify because they have a school alongside them.

The beauty of the view makes me appreciate how amazing and beautiful the parish community is. The longer I am in Chicago, the more familiar I become with the history of our parishes. I hear so many stories about the courageous, faith-filled immigrants who built so many of them and about their children who continued to build up the Church of Chicago. During my nearly three years here, I have visited about 300—or two-thirds—of these parishes and have had the opportunity to meet the current parishioners. Some of these parishes are primarily black or Hispanic, while others serve young urban professionals. Still others minister to the original ethnic groups that built them. There is a constant flow of diverse people in and out of the parishes that comprise this local Church.

Parishes are at the heart of the Church's life. They carry on the fundamental task, the basic mission of the Church, which, quite simply, is proclaiming the Lord Jesus and his Gospel. They are the places people go to find the living Gospel, the places where God meets his people each Sunday at his altar.

Like you, we in the archdiocese are looking toward the future of the parishes. As a matter of fact, I had an all-day meeting yesterday with our episcopal vicars and deans. We spent most of our time discussing our parishes—the things we think need to be done.

New circumstances raise new questions and present new challenges: consolidation, expansion, new forms of ministry, new parochial structures. All of these are issues we must confront if we want to keep the Church alive and vital. Sunday after Sunday, whether we are male or female, lay, religious, or clerical, black, Hispanic, Asian, or white, each of us gathers at the altar of a parish to worship the living God, to be nourished by his Word and sacraments, to experience Christian fellowship.

I am very grateful for your concern and your assistance in helping us strengthen the parishes and parish life. I can assure you that the results of this conference will be taken into account in Chicago as we plan for the future.

Now, if you will permit me, I would like to offer a prayer asking God's blessing for this meeting. We thank you, Lord our God, for the gift of each parish community. We also thank you for making it possible for this group of dedicated Catholics to reflect on and discuss ways of revitalizing and deepening parish life. I call upon you, Lord Jesus Christ, to send your spirit upon these disciples of yours. Help them to listen well, not only to each other but also to your Word. Help them to examine issues of mutual concern in an atmosphere of respect, charity, and fidelity. Give them the courage to make decisions that will enable parishes to be vital manifestations of your Church, carrying out your mission in the world. Amen.

DR. BUTLER: Thank you, Cardinal Bernardin. As you know, this parish study was funded through the Lilly Endowment. We are very fortunate to have with us Mr. Fred L. Hofheinz, who represents the Lilly Endowment and serves on FADICA's board of directors.

MR. HOFHEINZ: It is a distinct pleasure for me on behalf of the Lilly Endowment to welcome you to this consultation on the American Catholic Parish in Transition. Since this occasion marks the first public discussion of the Notre Dame study on American parish life, it represents, I think, an ideal forum for highlighting the importance of solid scholarly research into the contemporary American religious scene and the importance of foundation support for such activities.

My colleagues here from FADICA and the rest of the foundation community are aware, I suspect, that the Lilly Endowment in recent years has come to appreciate more and more the particular opportunities for philanthropic activity that are available in the research arena. Unlike other FADICA members, Lilly is an ecumenical foundation whose interest in religion spans all of American Christianity, not just Catholicism. Our research teams, accordingly, range all across the landscape of American religious life. In addition to this study of the contemporary Catholic parish, we are sponsoring inquiries into the contemporary Protestant parish and the contemporary Jewish congregation.

We liken our research program in religion to a kind of early warning system that can help illumine the landscape of things to come. We attempt to highlight the issues that need study now in order to produce data that will assist strategic planners in the 1990s. The Lilly Endowment is honored to have been able to provide the funds to support this inquiry.

DR. BUTLER: Thank you, Mr. Hofheinz. This symposium is one in a series of national conferences cosponsored by FADICA on contemporary trends and developments within the Catholic Church. It may come as a surprise to some that foundations do more than award grants. Foundations have become catalytic intermediaries, brokering discussions and stimulating new collaborative ventures within the Church. More and more they are becoming active agencies, taking the initiative not only to become better informed about issues and challenges facing the Church, but also to bring people together, promoting more collaboration and better planning.

As increasing numbers of the Catholic laity attain affluence and influence, their potential for affecting the course of Catholic life and directing its future will be all the greater. This potential can be realized to the extent that they are well informed, exposed to the most creative thinking within the Church, and work together. Meetings like this one have played an important role in providing FADICA members with the kind of ongoing education, interaction, and independent counsel that will enable them to make a responsible and lasting contribution to the Church.

We will see in this study many forms of lay initiative emerging at the parish level. I submit, however, that a developing self-identity as Church, which underlies this promising phenomena locally, manifests itself within the Catholic foundation and donor community as well. We too understand the implications of our baptism. We too want to bring our charisms and gifts to bear upon the work of the Church. It is in this spirit that we cosponsor this forum.

Our primary aim in this meeting is to help introduce the Notre Dame Study of Catholic Parish Life to our foundation members. In so doing, we hope to draw greater attention throughout the Church to this valuable examination. We will strive to broaden our understanding of parish needs in the pivotal areas of organization, leadership and staffing, parish worship, and spirituality.

We in FADICA are acutely interested in renewal, change, and a deepening of Catholic parish life. Fr. Tom Kleissler of RENEW, who is with us this morning, and other parish renewal pioneers can testify to the strong involvement of Catholic foundations in their work. The transformation of the Church into the kind of community envisioned by Vatican II hinges heavily upon the future of the parish. Because of the critical role of this institution, we are eager to find out where 20 years of reform and rapid social mobility have taken the American Catholic parish. What is the quality of leadership and the quality of participation? What ministries do parishes perform well? Where do they fall short of meeting people's needs? We look forward to exploring these questions with you. So let us begin.

CONCLUSION

FR. MURNION: Let me begin with a word about Frank Butler, president of FADICA, and his more-than-able assistant, Ann Pitcher. Anyone whom Frank and Ann have hosted knows what it is like to be graciously hosted. They make you feel that they care about you, respect you, and they make sure you have the tools necessary to do the job you came to do. They do all this with a real touch of class. I am grateful to them.

I should add that those of us who are not members of FADICA are also grateful to FADICA and most especially to the Lilly Endowment, whose interest and support made the Notre Dame study possible.

Obviously, there are many ways to look at Catholics and their parishes. We all brought to this conference certain experiences and ideas that influence our perception of parish life. Further, the last two days have reminded us that parishes are an expression of culture. They arise out of a set of beliefs, ways of thinking, ways of talking, ways of doing things—dressing, measuring time. Parishes have structures of programs and activities; they have rites of worship and celebration; they have patterns of leadership. It is culture that makes a parish.

This study confirms the dramatic changes that have occurred in parish life. There have been major changes in structure, leadership, and practice; perhaps, we are on the threshold of a broader transition, as significant as any of the changes of the past. Some have used the term *voluntary* to characterize the modern parish. However, with the passage of the years we may find another term that fits the reality better. While *voluntary* works well in creating a demand on us in the present, the outline of the new era in parish life is far from clear.

As Dr. Dolan reminded us, this is not the first time of transition for the American parish. We have been through it before, and we have adapted before. In a sense, all this change reveals the stability that underlies change. There has been remarkable consistency in the functions and services of parishes over the years, which is to be acknowledged and celebrated. Given Americans' skepticism about institutions, it is remarkable how faithful they have been to the parish. According to Gallup studies, the parish is the institution Catholics most respect. Moreover, despite misgivings about the quality of his leadership, the pastor is the "official" they most respect. While people always hope services will improve, they have enormous regard for the altruism of parochial leadership.

The Notre Dame study has emphasized certain areas that require attention, such as the basic attitude we as Catholics have toward life. Are we in it for ourselves, or can we make sacrifices that will reflect the communal sense, the sense of belonging to a community whose life and vitality we value?

Second, the matter of leadership keeps coming up. Who is to exercise leadership? How are they to exercise leadership? What training will be provided? What resources will be made available? Who will pay the bill?

Third, we have come to understand that good worship is not a matter of changing language or furniture. There are serious questions of quality with regard to preaching, music, style of celebration, and arrangement of space. We must create a climate of faith and mutual support, even when we are not feeling very worshipful in our hearts.

With regard to education, we need to offer values that really motivate people in their selection of schools and support for religious education. How little respect we professionals give the layperson's sincere efforts! How much we are inclined to attribute the worst motives to people when they go to confession or send their children to school. Take, for example, the belief that attending Mass is merely a matter of duty for the laity. There is a terrible tendency for people in leadership to underrate the motives and the quality of faith of those in our parishes.

The corporate notion of belonging despite who we are, what we do, what gender we are, whether we are successful or unsuccessful, that corporate sense of common worth that is part of our tradition must be protected with great care. A study like this one reveals not only what has happened intentionally but also what has happened unintentionally. We have to take responsibility for those changes that came about in spite of our wishes.

It seems clear to me that considerable effort should go into providing leadership training for all, including diocesan personnel. There is a tendency at all levels in the Church to blame the problems on those at a lower level—the so-called pecking order—and to say that people at those levels need training. While the primary reason for the erosion of parish life has not been conditions in the parish, it is likely that the parish will bear the brunt of responding to this erosion.

Let me conclude with a story. One of the best tales about good preaching I know came from a man named Patrick Henry, who was indeed a descendent of *the* Patrick Henry. This man's father, retiring as minister of a Texas parish he had served all his professional life, was asked what had made his preaching so effective. He said he wanted to think about it, and he came back the next day with a little bag of books.

"First of all," he began, reaching in and taking out the Bible, "you have to know the Word of God so thoroughly that it is your own word." Next he pulled out a book of biography. "I read a lot of biography," he said. "You get a sense of one life being lived from beginning to end and what life meant to that individual." Then he reached in his bag and brought out a history book. "People don't live their lives in a vacuum. I read history to understand the currents in which individual lives are lived." With a wink he added, "In preaching you also try to give people a fresh perspective on familiar things. What does that is humor." He took out a book of humor and placed it on the stack. Reaching in for the last book, a book of poetry, he said, "Good preaching offers a deeper look into what is very ordinary. These are the elements that have made my preaching effective all these years."

Some such mysterious mix gives us hope that what began with such a rush of the Spirit 20 years ago at Vatican II will be fulfilled according to the guidance of the Spirit in the years ahead, if we will just remain faithful to that Spirit.

APPENDIX II

THE U.S. PARISH
TWENTY YEARS AFTER
VATICAN II:
AN INTRODUCTION
TO THE STUDY

David C. Leege
Director, Center for the Study of Contemporary Society

Joseph Gremillion
Notre Dame Study of Catholic Parish Life

The Notre Dame Study of Catholic Parish Life is an interdisciplinary endeavor to understand better the American parish of the 1980s as a dynamic community. Many elements of parish life are addressed: organization, staffing, leadership, priorities, and their interrelations; liturgies and sacramental preparation; programs and participation; beliefs, values, expectations, and practices; historical, ethnographic, sociological, and religio-cultural contexts. The study is proceeding in three phases, 1981 to 1988.

PHASE I, 1981–1982
THE BROAD VIEW

To launch the study a broad probe sought to discover how a comprehensive analysis of American parish life could be undertaken. Ten percent of the nation's 18,500 parishes (at that time) were mailed questionnaires asking about staffing, structure, composition, and programmatic life. Of the 1,850 parishes receiving this request, over 1,100 answered. The respondent for each parish was a pastor or a knowledgeable parish administrator. The 60% rate of usable responses exceeds by far usual levels of cooperation to questionnaires received by mail. It indicated that American parishes are open to being studied and to self-evaluation. These responses also provided preliminary data from which a deeper study could be designed for a smaller sample of carefully chosen parishes.

The results from Phase I suggested a rich mosaic of parish life. There has been substantial but uneven adaptation to the climate of change suggested by the Second Vatican Council. Parish viability was not necessarily related to the incorporation of specific changes. Clearly lay leadership was well begun within the pastoral ministries of the parish but the new mechanisms of governance had not yet clearly formed. Expectations of lay participation in liturgies were widespread but some of the forms—music, responses—left much to be desired.

American Catholic parishes differed greatly by region, by religious majority/minority status, by urban/rural location, by ethnicity, by size, by structural complexity, and by dynamism of programs and loyalties. What the study needed was not simply statistical tables summarizing the general findings for the country. Instead it needed to penetrate further into the dynamics of each type of parish.

The Phase I study directors convened consultations with experts from appropriate disciplines, and more important, with persons in varying configurations of pastoral ministries at parish, diocesan, and national levels. These consultants advised on priorities for deeper study, on ways to develop appropriate samples of parishes and peoples, and on methods of data collection.

Phase I had incorporated the vision and ecclesial contacts of Rev.

Theodore M. Hesburgh, CSC, president of the University of Notre Dame, and Msgr. John J. Egan, director of Notre Dame's Institute for Pastoral and Social Ministry. They added to the team the wide experience and research understanding of Rev. Philip Murnion, former director of "The Parish Project" conducted under the Committee on the Parish of the National Conference of Catholic Bishops from 1977 to 1982, and the skills of Prof. Michael Welch of Notre Dame's sociology department.

Armed with the Phase I findings, Murnion and Egan assembled a Phase II research team and acquired major funding from the Lilly Endowment, Inc., which had already supported Phase I. (The Lilly Endowment has been a significant benefactor for the research and theological training efforts of America's religious organizations.)

PHASE II, 1983–1985
IN-DEPTH STUDY
THROUGH MULTIPLE APPROACHES

The parish study combines in a unique manner several approaches to parish studies. Most previous research surveyed beliefs, attitudes, and practices of parishioners; in a few cases parish structure in a single parish or a couple of parishes has been examined. But no study had as yet systematically investigated both basic areas in the context of liturgical practices and historical developments across a wide variety of parishes.

The first unique quality of the current Notre Dame study is that it combines analysis of parish structure, leadership, and performance with study of parishioners' views and behavior. This is accomplished by surveys and interviews with parish leaders (pastor, paid staff, and volunteer lay leaders), together with scientific sample surveys of members of the same parish. The findings can be correlated in great detail via computer.

A second unique factor is the interdisciplinary character of the research: it involves sociology and history, liturgy, doctrine, and theology, together with organizational analysis and community power studies, parishioners' beliefs, practices, and communal faith experiences, past and present.

A third significant element is that Phase II's in-depth study focuses on a sample of 36 parishes chosen as representative of the 1,100 parishes who responded to our preliminary questionnaires of Phase I. Based on the original findings, the U.S. Church was divided into six sociocultural and ecclesial regions. From each of these regions six parishes were chosen as representative of that region, according to criteria of rural, small town, suburban, and urban; size, composition, and organizational complexity; dynamism of activities, leadership, and participation; and ethnic background.

Spanish-speaking parishes were not included because Hispanic Catholicism has such unique qualities that a scientific team, field researchers, computer encoders, and others who know Spanish and Hispanic religio-culture would have been needed. Also, Spanish copies of all survey materials would have been necessary. It is hoped that a specific study of Spanish-speaking parishes of the United States might be launched in the near future.

This complex sample design yields sufficient cases to generalize about each of the 36 parishes with a high degree of accuracy. But it also allows for valid comparison of different types of parishes. And through weighting procedures, it generates accurate and valid findings for all non-Hispanic Catholics in the United States *within their parishes*. Previous national studies of Catholics have relied heavily on general sample surveys of the adult U.S. population. Or, local studies have addressed one or a handful of parishes.

This study is based on surveys of parish membership lists, that is, people known to be Catholics within each sampled parish. Its results, then, will not be so accurate for inactive or apostate Catholics; however, they will be more accurate than previous national studies for the core Catholic population that each parish serves regularly. An important principle guiding the study is that understanding Catholics is not merely an exercise in comparing percentages in national survey tables. It requires comparing Catholics *within the context* of their local parishes, for it is within parishes that we are baptized and come to learn about God, we marry and raise families, we enjoy friends and argue about programs, we offer our help or shirk our responsibilities, and we die.

A final significant element involves the many methods of data collection utilized during the investigative period from April 1983 to November 1984.

1. Two-person teams, composed of a liturgist and a social scientist, were assigned to each parish for on-site visits. Once recruited, these specialists, sixteen in number, came to Notre Dame for lengthy training sessions in September 1983.

2. Four separate questionnaires were elaborated and field tested: for pastors, paid professional staff, volunteer lay leaders, and parishioners. The number of pages in each instrument, respectively, is 37, 38, 37, and 34; completion time ranged between two and four hours each. These were mailed to the 36 pastors and directly to 117 staff, 262 volunteer leaders, and 4,555 scientifically selected parishioners at their individual residences. (A pretest had shown that for this type of study, a mailout procedure was more reliable than using the parish as a distribution and collection point.) Volunteer leaders and staff were selected both for the important positions they occupy in the parish structure and for the influence over parish activities they were reputed to exert. Usable responses were encouraged by at least four direct contacts with each sampled individual and are exceptionally high for this type of research: pastors, 94%; paid staff, 76%; volunteer leaders, 77%; and ordinary parishioners, 59%.

3. Three other instruments were prepared for the on-site visits. These helped the liturgist and sociologist to describe the physical layout of the

parish church and changes since 1964; to record observations of regular weekend Masses; and to interview decision makers regarding liturgical planning, sacramental preparation, and guidance from diocesan or other local sources.

4. The field staff members were given guidelines not only for their interviews and observations but also for the collection of historical documents. Visits were made between October and December 1983 by the team, for an average of 7.5 specialist days in each parish. All field staff members have at least a master's degree in their specialities, and many hold the doctorate.

5. Ethnographic and historical accounts for each parish were prepared by the field staff. These were based on time samplings of bulletins and newsletters, school materials, jubilee volumes and other historical records, and interviews with knowledgeable parish leaders. They describe the parish influence structure, the parish's place in the life of the larger local community, and its most positive and negative features in the minds of knowledgeable local people.

6. At the same time a group of six historians, also holding doctorates, were trained to collect other materials for parish life histories in each U.S. region. Each has prepared a 120–150 page monograph on the history of Catholic parishes in his region. The monographs examine such areas as parish locales, size, ethnicity, role of laity, clerical leadership, organizational complexity and parish priorities, popular pieties, religious socialization and education, and ecumenical orientations.

The Program for Research on Religion, Church, and Society of the Center for the Study of Contemporary Society, has been responsible for Phase II of the parish study. Dr. David Leege, a political scientist and director of this research center, exercises overall direction of Phase II and heads its professional research team of three other specialists: Dr. Michael Welch, associate professor, sociology department; Dr. Jay Dolan, director of the Cushwa Center for the Study of American Catholicism, and associate professor, history department; and Dr. Mark Searle, associate director of the Center for Pastoral Liturgy, 1979–1983, and now director of liturgical studies, theology department. In addition to the sociological, liturgical, and historical field staffs, approximately 40 Notre Dame graduate and undergraduate students, and religious and priests on sabbatical have been utilized as coders and data analysts.

Msgr. Egan, who is now director of the Office of Human Relations and Ecumenism, Archdiocese of Chicago, and Rev. Murnion, now director of the newly formed National Pastoral Life Center in New York City, remain as active consultants to the Phase II research team.

PHASE III, 1984–1988
PASTORAL INTERPRETATION
AND APPLICATIONS

Msgr. Joseph Gremillion, who in 1983 succeeded Msgr. Egan as director of Notre Dame's Institute for Pastoral and Social Ministry, now directs the pastoral interpretation phase of the study in collaboration with Leege and Murnion. During the past year the three have worked together, in consultation with pastoral leaders around the country, to plan an agenda of analysis, communication, and feedback. A major concern has been the proper interface between research and pastoral interpretation so that Church leaders themselves will draw out the study's many implications for policy at appropriate levels.

Results will be released and interpreted through a variety of mechanisms.

1. Over the next two years, approximately every two months a press notice and a background report of about a dozen pages will be released by the University of Notre Dame's Office of Public Information. The reports will systematically present and interpret findings in the topical areas addressed by the study. Reports typically will be prepared by Dr. Leege and Msgr. Gremillion, with the help of other staff members and consultants. The reports are aimed at interested church leaders as well as other publics.

2. A wide variety of scholarly papers, journal articles, dissertations, monographs, and books will appear over the next six years. Generally, these will be written by the Phase II research staff and their students. They are directed to scientific and professional audiences in sociology, history, theology (both liturgical and pastoral), psychology, and political science. The six historical monographs prepared under Dr. Dolan's direction will be the first to be published. Following the initial phases of data analysis, the study directors intend to open their data archives to sociologists of religion, theologians, and historians located outside Notre Dame so that findings may enter the scholarly mainstream more rapidly.

3. Each parish that participated in the study will receive a profile comparing the beliefs, expectations, and practices of its people with those of U.S. Catholics across all 36 parishes. The profiles may be helpful to each parish in planning its ministries as well as assisting neighboring parishes. These reports reflect the deep gratitude the study directors feel to these parishes in opening themselves for serious study and in giving so much of their time for the overall quality of American parish life.

4. Perhaps the most important aspect of Phase III concerns the pastoral interpretation of findings. Msgr. Gremillion and Dr. Leege hope to avoid the usual syndrome of such studies where an expert says, "This is the way it is, and the Church had better adjust." Instead we will try to disseminate information in a way that the Church at all levels provides interpretation of its meaning and draws whatever conclusions are appro-

priate to its local parish purposes. Thus a large variety of conferences, symposia, and workshops is anticipated. While a small portion of the Lilly Endowment grant will initiate these efforts, many Catholic organizations, dioceses, and foundations will share in the responsibilities of data dissemination and pastoral interpretation.

A. The first major national conference occurred in Chicago in late May 1985 under the sponsorship and direction of FADICA, the association of Foundations and Donors Interested in Catholic Activities, Inc., with headquarters in Washington, D.C. Similar to recent topical conferences FADICA has convened on vocations and applied research in the Church, this conference drew implications from the Notre Dame Study of Catholic Parish Life for understanding the parish in post-Vatican II transition: changing patterns in leadership style, staffing, structure, and service; changing expectations of pastors; emerging patterns of worship and spirituality. Some of the presenters and panelists were study staff members but most were drawn from the larger Church. FADICA invited about 100 people, including officials within its membership, key bishops, and NCCB staff concerned with parish programs, and pastoral specialists from associations, seminaries, dioceses, and parishes.

B. Following shorter sessions with the leadership of a larger archdiocese and a smaller diocese, a series of regional meetings will be hosted by major dioceses around the country during 1985 and 1986. While attention will again be focused on findings from the study, interpretations will be offered primarily by people responsible for parish ministries.

C. From 1985 through 1988 numerous Catholic organizations will concentrate portions of their annual conventions, training workshops, reports, and publications on the Notre Dame Study of Catholic Parish Life. Those will include organizations concerned with parish leadership, liturgy, social ministry, retreats, priestly formation, education, and many functional ministries.

D. Still other methods for dissemination and pastoral interpretation are being explored. For example, based on its study experience the research team is seeking ways to develop instruments and friendly computer software for local parish self-study. In the era of microcomputers and personal computers, many parishes are now acquiring technology that could be used for self-study and informed problem solving, as well as parish censuses, payrolls, and tax reports. The use of videocassettes and teleconferencing is also under study, since the University of Notre Dame has recently acquired technical means and production staff appropriate to these media.

TOPICS AND AREAS OF FUTURE REPORTS

As the bimonthly reports are released over the next two years, readers can expect each of the following aspects of parish life to be addressed by one or more reports. Often the reports will offer "different lenses" (i.e., contrast the views and approaches of pastors, staff, volunteer leaders, and ordinary parishioners). They will also examine regional, urban/rural ethnic, and parish size differences.

1. Membership, participation, and activities—relationships in parish life, entry or departure, identification, family and ethnicity, activities beyond liturgies that attract participation, who is and isn't thought to be a Catholic.

2. Leadership—pastoral, staff, and lay leadership: selection, training, roles and styles, parish councils and parish governance, policy making, pastor-staff-lay consensus and conflict, diocesan relations.

3. Liturgy and spirituality—planning and preparation, styles, participation, music, preaching, religious meaning in rite, liturgical content and pieties, Marian and family devotions, personal prayer life.

4. Parish as community—loyalty and attachment, community as sacrament, popular expectations for parish ministries, priorities, and staff capabilities, social and fraternal organizations, friendship patterns, smaller groups, alienation, communication and networks.

5. Parish and outside community—social ministry and social action, social and political issues, teaching authority of the Church on economic and political affairs, culture and politics, ecumenical relations.

6. Religious education, formation, and beliefs—parish educational programs: schools, catechesis, youth, adult education; extraparish religious education; doctrinal theology and operative theology, foundational religious beliefs, views of God, Jesus, Church, sacraments; views of change in the Church.

7. Budgets and finances—giving patterns and their causes; planning, policy making and budget authority; financial management.

ABOUT THE SPEAKERS

DR. DAVID C. LEEGE is senior research director of the Notre Dame Study of Catholic Parish Life. A political scientist and consultant to governments and universities, Dr. Leege is professor of government, director of the Program for Research on Religion, Church and Society, and, primarily, director of the Center for the Study of Contemporary Society at the University of Notre Dame. He has authored a wide range of publications including such diverse topics as religion and politics, research methods and measurement, voting behavior, and higher education administration and policy.

DR. JAY P. DOLAN is associate professor of history and director of the Charles and Margaret Hall Cushwa Center for the Study of American Catholicism at the University of Notre Dame. He is also the past director of the historical research section for the Notre Dame Study of Catholic Parish Life. Listed in *American Catholic Who's Who* (23rd edition), *Who's Who in the Midwest,* and *Directory of American Scholars,* Dr. Dolan is also the author of numerous books, articles, newsletters, and essays, as well as a noted lecturer and conference presider.

REV. THOMAS F. VENTURA is the vicar for priests in the Archdiocese of Chicago. He has served in various capacities from associate pastor and faculty member to dean of formation and copastor of a team ministry project. Fr. Ventura has also been a member of the Clergy Personnel Board of Chicago, chairman of the Association of Chicago Priests, board member of the La Grange Human Relations Commission, and member of the Evanston Police Citizens' Advisory Board.

REV. PHILIP J. MURNION is currently the director of the Pastoral Life Conference of the Archdiocese of New York, the office for continuing education of the clergy. He is also the director of the newly created National Pastoral Life Center, which provides information, consulting, and training resources for dioceses, as well as the editor of the new quarterly *CHURCH.* Fr. Murnion also serves as adjunct professor at Fordham University and as associate pastor of Our Lady of Loreto Parish and the Holy Name Center for Homeless Men in Manhattan. He has written and lectured widely on parish life, ministry, and social ministry.

DR. MARK SEARLE, who holds a doctorate from Trier, Germany, is presently the assistant professor of theology at the University of Notre Dame, a post he has held for two years. Dr. Searle taught liturgy and sacramental theology in Canterbury, England, prior to taking up an assignment at Notre Dame's Center for Pastoral Liturgy. He is a renowned author of five books and countless essays, collections, and publications, as well as an accomplished public speaker in the areas of sacramental theology and conversion and the catechumenate.

Typeface
Bembo

Typography
Automated Graphic Systems
White Plains, Maryland